T0190783

# THE WHISKEY SOUR

# THE
# WHISKEY
# SOUR

**A MODERN
GUIDE TO THE
CLASSIC COCKTAIL**

---

## JEANETTE HURT

UNIVERSITY PRESS OF KENTUCKY

Published by the University Press of Kentucky, scholarly publisher
for the Commonwealth, serving Bellarmine University, Berea College,
Centre College of Kentucky, Eastern Kentucky University, The Filson
Historical Society, Georgetown College, Kentucky Historical Society,
Kentucky State University, Morehead State University, Murray State
University, Northern Kentucky University, Spalding University,
Transylvania University, University of Kentucky, University of Louisville,
University of Pikeville, and Western Kentucky University.
All rights reserved.

*Editorial and Sales Offices:* The University Press of Kentucky
663 South Limestone Street, Lexington, Kentucky 40508-4008
www.kentuckypress.com

Illustrations by Arthur Balitskii, Aurelija Diliute, DiViArt, Nataliia Machula,
Andreeva Marina, Svitlana Medvedieva, Netkoff, NikitinaArt, Dmytro
Nychytalyuk, Ilya Oktyabr, peintre_mari, Qualit Design, Polina Raulina, Padma
Sanjaya, Victoria Sergeeva, Dasha Soma, Bodor Tivadar, and Irina Trusova.

Cataloging-in-Publication data is available from the Library of Congress.

ISBN 978-1-9859-0089-9 (hardcover : alk. paper)
ISBN 978-1-9859-0091-2 (epub)
ISBN 978-1-9859-0090-5 (pdf)

This book is printed on acid-free paper meeting
the requirements of the American National Standard
for Permanence in Paper for Printed Library Materials.

Manufactured in the United States of America.

ASSOCIATION
of UNIVERSITY
PRESSES

Member of the Association
of University Presses

*To Toni Senglaub, whose favorite cocktail is the whiskey sour,*
*and to Tamara Johnston and Chris Gluesing,*
*who have supported all my book endeavors over the years.*

*Cheers!*

# CONTENTS

# Introduction

The whiskey sour doesn't have the sophisticated cachet of the Manhattan. It doesn't have the historical allure of the old-fashioned. It doesn't even have the regional panache of the mint julep. And it's not as "in the moment" as the boulevardier.

The whiskey sour might be the most underrated whiskey cocktail. It's not stirred in a sexy glass pitcher, and its name is as straightforward as they come, but what it lacks in marketing appeal it makes up for in drinkability.

"It's kind of the pizza of whiskey cocktails," says Dave Colt, owner of Sun King Brewery and Distillery in Indianapolis. "It appeals to all sorts of palates, and it's sort of an entrée into more complex whiskey drinks. When it's made right, it's a beautiful thing, and when it's made wrong, it's still a good thing."

The whiskey sour appeals to whiskey connoisseurs as well as to twenty-one-year-olds drinking legally for the first time. "It's a gateway cocktail, the dipping your toes into the waters when it comes to whiskey or scotch cocktails," says Jane Danger, a mixologist who designs cocktails for Pernod Ricard brands, including Glenlivet. "It's also a gateway for building off of, a platform to plug other things into. It's like your mother sauce, and you can take it and really have fun with it."

"A whiskey sour is as classic as you get," says Ross Salchow, former marketing director of Great Lakes Distillery in Milwaukee. "It's genuinely got such a wide appeal."

According to Peter Kalleward, mixologist for Destination Kohler in Kohler, Wisconsin, the whiskey sour is one of the first five drinks he teaches new bartenders. "We might make zero whiskey sours for two nights in a row, but then the next night, we'll make eight," he says. "It's not a cocktail that's ever gone out of style." The whiskey sour, "like the old-fashioned, is a great starting point," Kalleward says. "It's like a canvas. You start with the basic ingredients, and then you can run with it."

Like the Manhattan and the old-fashioned, it's a deceptively simple cocktail. If you have quality ingredients on hand, the whiskey sour is deliciously easy to make. "It's absolutely one of my favorite drinks," says Myra Bargainer, founder of Paul Sutton Bourbon. "If you use fresh ingredients, it's just a fantastic cocktail."

But unlike the Manhattan and the old-fashioned, very few people hate the whiskey sour. Some people can take it or leave it, but a whole lot of people love the whiskey sour with a passion. You'll find it in the swankiest cocktail bars and Michelin-starred restaurants, but you'll also find it at backyard barbecues and dive bars. This easily quaffed cocktail is sometimes overlooked, but it's time to give this elegant classic its proper recognition.

The whiskey sour boasts a heritage that stretches back nearly two centuries. Yet its history is largely inaccurate, and if you do an online search of its origins, the story you stumble upon will most likely be erroneous. The whiskey sour's simplicity also belies its complexity. There are numerous formulas for this cocktail, and every recipe developer claims that his or hers is the best.

The whiskey sour also boasts some of the most interesting descendants of classic cocktails, as it has evolved into the Penicillin, the Gold Rush, and various smashes, all modern classics that can trace their ancestral roots back to the whiskey sour. You can riff on a Manhattan, switch up a boulevardier, or play off a julep, but all these whiskey cocktails remain fairly similar to their original recipes, whereas the whiskey sour's myriad spin-offs have become cocktails in their own right, different enough to have their own nomenclature and fans.

As you might have surmised, I have great affection for this beautiful cocktail. Like the perfect black dress, it is appropriate for any occasion, and it can be dressed up or dressed down. It can be served in the backyard or on the beach, at home or in the most elegant of places.

This book celebrates the rich history of the whiskey sour—its formulas, its riffs, and its deliciousness. Come along and rediscover this gorgeous classic.

## A Word on Whiskey and Other Branded Spirits

Some of the recipes in this book call for specific brands of bourbons, whiskeys, and ryes, as well as distinctive spirits and liqueurs. This is because the bartender or distiller who created the recipe has certain preferences and specified these brands. But that doesn't mean *you* have to use them. Although different brands have distinctive tastes—and sometimes these differences are notable—you don't have to run out to the liquor store for a particular brand every time you make a recipe from this book. In fact, if you have a favorite brand of whiskey that you keep stocked in your home bar, you should absolutely use it. The same goes for bitters and other ingredients as well.

Some of the drinks might be slightly altered if you use a different brand or a different product, such as substituting Cointreau for triple sec, but that's okay, as long as you like it. Most of the fine bartenders and distillers whose recipes are included in this book will not be offended if you make their cocktails according to your own tastes. They will simply be pleased that you are enjoying their creations.

So now, on to enjoying one of the best whiskey cocktails in the world!

# History of the Whiskey Sour

**A** **properly made whiskey sour is a delectable work** of art. It's a simple yet elegant beverage that boasts a long, long history. For nearly two centuries, people have been combining whiskey, sugar, and lemon juice in various proportions and in innumerable ways. While the old-fashioned is usually considered the oldest cocktail ever made, one could argue that sour cocktails are just as venerable, as their roots can be traced back to punch.

## A One, Two (Three, Four, Five) Punch

Long before the word *cocktail* graced our vocabulary, there was punch. The history of punch dates back to at least the 1600s, and it was probably drunk a lot earlier than that. David Wondrich details the drink's roots in his beloved book *Punch,* noting that the earliest written reference to punch was in a letter sent on September 28, 1632, from Robert Adams, who was stationed in India and worked for the British East India Company. Adams wrote, "I hop you will keep good house together and drincke punch by no allowance." This suggests that the recipient knew exactly what punch was and that drinking it was a common experience.

Although grog was developed around the same time, punch is the most likely ancestor of sour cocktails, including the whiskey sour. Punch probably originated in Asia and traveled to Europe with sailors and merchants. It may have been served in India, as the word *punch* is similar to the Sanskrit word *panch*, which means "five" and might refer to the number of traditional components of punch: sour, sweet, strong, weak, and spice. But as Wondrich notes in his book, punch can have five components or fifty, depending on the recipe, the circumstance, and what one considers a component.

There are frequent mentions of punch in the seventeenth and eighteenth centuries. By the early eighteenth century, it was an established alcoholic concoction. A British newspaper reported in 1703 on Sir Thomas Jefford's celebration of the coronation of Queen Anne. Besides ordering five cannons to be fired, he toasted to her health with "a Bumper of Punch, having ordered the same to be made and prepared in a large Copper containing 20 gallons."

The components came together in a well-known nineteenth-century rhyme that describes the basic properties of punch: "One of sour, two of sweet, three of strong, and four of weak." Several sources claim that this is the original recipe for punch, but it leaves out the fifth component: spice. This little ditty likely first appeared in 1896 in a widely published newspaper article about "A West Indies Appetizer." It states: "Falernum is a very delightful concoction which the West Indies [man] mindful of his health takes in sips and swallows at least once a day, and about an hour before his dinner. 'An appetizer,' he calls it. 'One of sour, two of sweet, three of strong, and four of weak,' such is the recipe as given by the West Indies housewife." The article goes on to explain the ingredients: sour is lime or lemon juice, sweet is sugar, strong is rum, and weak is water. In early punch recipes, tea might be substituted for water. The fifth element—spice—could be bitters or spices such as cinnamon or nutmeg.

Punch was tippled in punch houses, as well as in bars and saloons. Jerry Thomas, who is considered the father of American mixology, worked in saloons and featured seventy-nine punch recipes in his book *How to Mix Drinks, Or the Bon Vivant's Companion,* first published in 1862. The vast majority of his punch recipes featured brandy, rum, or gin, but six whiskey punches were included. His basic whiskey punch called for whiskey, water, and sugar, with a small piece of lemon or lemon rind. Except for the water, this is similar to a sour. His Irish whiskey punch is closer to the whiskey sour: "This is the genuine Irish beverage. It is generally made one-third part pure whiskey, two-thirds boiling water in which the sugar has been dissolved. If lemon punch, the rind is rubbed on the sugar, and a small portion of juice added before the whiskey is poured in."

Thomas's weren't the first punch recipes ever published. *Oxford Night Caps, Being a Collection of Receipts for Making Various Beverages Used in the University,* beat him to the punch (so to speak) with its initial publication in 1827 (republished in 1835 and 1847). It features a dozen punch recipes, including a lemon punch, which is similar to a white brandy sour, and a Leander punch, a concoction of whiskey, lemon juice, brandy, and ale.

Although saloons and punch houses served punches, they were more frequently enjoyed at home, where people did most of their drinking at the time. This means that most alcoholic beverages, including punches, were prepared by women, as detailed in the best-selling books of this era—household management manuals. Dozens were published throughout the nineteenth and early twentieth centuries, and any author worth her posset included recipes for punches, cordials, liqueurs, and spirit-laden desserts. Spirits and spirited concoctions were not just for entertaining; they were also used as remedies for illnesses and injuries.

Scottish writer and journalist Christian Isobel Johnstone used the pseudonym Mistress Margaret Dods to pen *The Cook and Housewife's Manual: A Practical System of Modern Cookery* in 1826. Besides information on Gloucester jelly for invalids and filbert butter, the last quarter of her book focuses on "Liqueurs, Cordials, Punch, Brandies, Possets, Made-Wines, and Household Beers." Her recipe for Glasgow punch, like Thomas's whiskey punch, sounds remarkably like a whiskey sour. Her recipe for Norfolk punch calls for the addition of oranges and orange juice, which are also included in some whiskey sour recipes.

Other household management books hinted at combining lemon, sugar, and spirits, including *The Kentucky Housewife*, published by Mrs. Lettice Bryan in 1839. Besides instructions on how to cook squirrel, she offered recipes for cordials made out of everything from roses to gooseberries. They all involved steeping the cordial's main ingredients for twenty-four hours in lukewarm water, then straining and adding sugar and brandy. She also included recipes for grape syrup, mint cordial, and cherry bounce, which all required "rectified whiskey." Her instructions for preserving lemon juice sound remarkably like the directions for making a sour cocktail—add sugar and white brandy to the juice before corking the bottle.

One of the most popular manuals of the nineteenth century was *The Book of Household Management* by Mrs. Isabella Beeton, published in 1861. If she were around today, her book would be feted by celebrities and all over social media. In her voluminous instructions she offered "General Observations on Beverages," including a spirited section that covers everything from spiced wines to ales to punches. Her punch recipes are quite similar to large-batch sour cocktails, and her treatise on lemonade sounds curiously like a sour cocktail. The lemonade was made with two lemon rinds, juice from three large or four small lemons, one pound of loaf sugar, and one quart of boiling water. The instructions are as follows: "Rub some of the sugar, in lumps on 2 of the lemons until they have imbibed all the oil from them, and put it with the remainder of the sugar into a jug; add the lemon-juice (but no pips), and pour over the whole a quart of boiling water. When the sugar is dissolved, strain the lemonade through a fine sieve or piece of muslin, and when cool, it will be ready for use." Mrs. Beeton also recommended two enhancements: "The lemonade will be much improved by having the white of an egg beaten up in it; a little sherry mixed with it, also, makes this beverage much nicer." These directions transform ordinary lemonade into a sherry sour.

Mrs. Beeton's recipe appeared, word for word, in the first edition of Jerry Thomas's book—the third recipe in his chapter on "Temperance Drinks." (Oddly, Thomas included two alcoholic lemonades in the chapter on nonalcoholic beverages, but perhaps the addition of sherry or a "dash of port wine" wasn't considered alcoholic back in the day.) Thomas's book came out a year after Beeton's, and he may have plagiarized her work. But Mrs. Beeton herself was likely guilty of plagiarism, as she lifted recipes from other books and, as a magazine writer, had readers send her their recipes, which she included in her best seller without credit. Thus, sherry sour lemonade might have been created by some unknown housewife.

What all these bartending manuals and household management books tell us is that punches and cordials were very popular and that these beverages were the likely precursors of sour cocktails and, more specifically, the whiskey sour.

## Cocktails Come of Age

Cocktails arrived on the scene in the 1800s, but they weren't the only game in town, and they weren't necessarily the most popular alcoholic concoctions. If order is an indication of importance, when Jerry Thomas's cocktail book first appeared in 1862, punches were listed first, followed by eggnogs and juleps, smashes, cobblers, and finally cocktails and crustas.

Smashes consisted of sugar, water, spirit, and mint with shaved ice, orange, and berries. The whiskey smash is listed third in Thomas's book (minus the orange and berries). Cobblers were made of fruit, sugar, and spirit shaken together with ice, but no herbs. "Crusta is made in the same way as a fancy cocktail, with a little lemon juice and a small lump of ice added," Thomas explained. Rub the rim of a "fancy red-wine glass" with a lemon slice, dip the rim in sugar, and insert an entire peel of lemon for decoration. "Then smile."

Fixes and sours come later in the book. A fix is basically sugar, water, lemon juice, and spirit stirred together and then "dressed with fruit in season." "A sour is made with the same ingredients as a [brandy] fix, omitting all fruits except a small piece of lemon, the

## A Brief History of Grog

Another citrusy beverage being served in the 1700s was grog. This concoction was developed by the British Navy and enjoyed primarily by sailors. They needed something to quench their thirst on long voyages, and freshwater stored in casks sometimes grew mildew or algae. The alternative, of course, was beer, wine, or spirits. (Back then, lots of people drank alcoholic beverages because of the scarcity of freshwater.) Sailors were initially rationed pints of beer, which was eventually replaced with spirits.

By the 1600s, rum was the spirit of choice for the British Navy. But too much rum led to drunk sailors, so in 1740 an intelligent admiral named Edward Vernon ordered that each sailor be given half a pint of booze mixed with a quart of water. The mixing was to be done "in one Scuttled Butt kept for that purpose and to be done upon Deck, and in the presence of the Lieutenant of the Watch, who is to see that the men are not defrauded of their allowance of Rum." The men were allowed to use "savings of their Salt Provisions and Bread [to] purchase Sugar and Limes to make the water more palatable to them." The sailors, who  referred to the admiral as "Old Grog" because of his heavy grogram cloak, eventually started to call this mixture of sugar, water, lime, and rum *grog*. Grog was served to British sailors until 1970, when the practice was discontinued.

If you think grog sounds a lot like punch or a sour cocktail, you're right. Although it existed around the same time as punch, grog didn't really catch on, so it's more of a cousin to the whiskey sour's historic ancestor.

juice of which must be pressed in the glass." The brandy fix is the 140th recipe in Thomas's book. Here are his instructions for making it:

**Brandy Fix**
(Use small bar glass.)
1 table-spoon of sugar. ½ a wine-glass of water.
¼ of a lemon. 1 do. [dry ounce] brandy.

Fill a tumbler two-thirds full of shaved ice. Stir with a spoon, and dress the top with fruit in season.

Curiously, one cocktail was conspicuously absent from the first edition of Thomas's book. He included several whiskey punches, a whiskey cocktail (known today as the old-fashioned), and even a whiskey crusta, but there was no whiskey sour or even a whiskey fix. Both brandy and gin sours and fixes were represented, but there was a notable absence of sours and fixes made with whiskey.

Dozens of articles, some written by major spirit and wine publications, cite the first edition of Thomas's book as being the first to publish a whiskey sour recipe, but that's not true. The first edition of his bartending classic contained absolutely no mention of this classic cocktail; the second edition, which came out in 1876, also omitted it. Only in the third edition, published in 1887—two years after Thomas died—did a whiskey sour recipe appear. The publisher wanted to incorporate popular drinks of the 1880s, so the whiskey sour was added to page 40, after the gin sour but before the brandy sour and the Jersey sour. This edition also contains a whiskey fix, which indicates the growing popularity of whiskey cocktails. It's also interesting to note that by the third

> ## The Posthumous Whiskey Sour—1887 Edition
>
> **Whiskey Sour**
> (Use small bar-glass.)
> Take 1 large tea-spoonful of powdered white sugar,
> dissolved in a little Seltzer or Apollinaria water [a natural
> sparkling water].
> The juice of half a small lemon.
> 1 wine-glass of Bourbon or rye whiskey.
> Fill the glass full of shaved ice, shake up and strain into a
> claret glass. Ornament with berries.
>
> Thomas's gin sour was "dressed" with orange or pineapple
> and berries, and the brandy sour was "ornamented" with
> orange and berries, but the recipes were otherwise the same
> as the whiskey sour.

edition, these drinks were shaken rather than stirred,
reflecting the evolution of sour cocktails.

## Before Thomas: The Whiskey Sour in Print

The third edition of Thomas's *How to Mix Drinks* was the
first *book* to include a recipe for the whiskey sour, but the
cocktail's origins can be traced further back. By the time
a recipe appears in a book, it has usually been around
for a while, and the history of the whiskey sour can be
followed through many nineteenth-century newspapers.

Several sources claim an article published on
January 4, 1870, in a Wisconsin newspaper, the *Waukesha
Plain Dealer,* was the first printed reference to a whiskey
sour. A story about a man and his cousin drinking at a
bar and playing billiards with a Methodist mentioned
it: "'Amen,' says the Methodist, as he ordered another

whisky sour." However, there are a number of earlier printed references to the drink.

Perhaps the earliest was an article published in Mississippi, in the *Natchez Newspaper and Public Advertiser* on November 29, 1826. It is basically a listing of addictions, and it names the whiskey sour in a rant about alcoholic drinks:

> There is your rum, brandy, gin, whiskey, wine, tody, and julep slaves, these must be multiplied, the genera by the various species of each, of which there are ramifications innumerable as the sands, as a short specimen take whiskey strong, whiskey sweet, whiskey sour and sweet, sweet and sour, bitter and sweet, sweet and bitter; hot and cold, flip and tody, Irish country, barley, rye, potato, wheat or oaten, malted and unsalted, Monongahela, German and Smoked, and you have a part only of the species of a single genera, each holding its particular subjects bound down in chains of servility more abject and more brutalizing than tongue or pen can describe.

Another early printed reference was a hot toddy recipe that is remarkably similar to the whiskey sour. This recipe suggests that the cocktail is related to hot drinks, which, given the ingredients, makes sense. The *Vermont Patriot and State Gazette* in Montpelier published the following recipe on January 16, 1832:

> "This Cold,"—Messrs. Editors.—Having been severely afflicted by "this cold," I beg to offer the following recipe as one of the best and most agreeable remedies. One dose will

generally relieve the patient—two will check
the distemper—the third will quite restore him.
N. B. Ladies may substitute old port for whiskey.
Recipe.—Take one lemon and squeeze it into
Half pint tumbler, add to this two ounces of
good brown, or loaf sugar; to this put sixteen
thimbles full of old rye whiskey and *quad. suff.*
[enough] of boiling water—to be taken on going
to bed—add an extra blanket, and keep quiet till
it operates.

By the 1860s and 1870s, the whiskey sour was so
established that newspapers frequently mentioned it,
often to make a point about a person's character. For
example, in New York, the *Buffalo Commercial* reported
on September 3, 1868: "The leading drink to-day among
the Democrats, after hearing the news from Vermont
is 'whiskey sour.'" It was equally popular among the
customers at Mike Norton's on Coney Island. The *New
York Herald* reported on July 12, 1876, that, along with
sherry cobblers, the whiskey sour was a favorite tipple
there.

In reporting on a Baltimore bank robbery on August
22, 1872, the *Richmond Times Dispatch* pointed out just
how popular the whiskey sour was. The robber's "companion is described as a short, thick-set man, about the
same height. . . . He also dressed well, and was a great
lover of 'whiskey sour,' or as the drink at this season
of the year is more generally known, 'lime punch.'"
This further establishes the link between punches and
whiskey sours.

The whiskey sour's popularity had spread to Europe
by the 1870s. On July 12, 1873, a Virginia newspaper, the
*Alexandria Gazette,* published a story about American

drinks in Vienna, as reported by the *Baltimore American*'s Vienna correspondent. The story provides "a list of the plain American drinks" that were popular, served with crushed ice. Among the seven whiskey cocktails was the whiskey sour. Another story, published in England's *Leicester Chronicle* on November 8, 1879, was headlined: "Holiday Notes by Local Tourists. Paris and Back on a Bicycle." It reports, "In the window of one of the cafés near Madeleine Church was displayed a list of American drinks." The list included five whiskey cocktails, including the whiskey sour.

Casual readers in the nineteenth century readily recognized the whiskey sour, and a story published on August 28, 1873, in the *Vermont Standard* reveals that most people were also familiar with its ingredients. The paper published a complete listing of "the 'stationery account' of D. P. Lowe, member of Congress from Kansas," and noted that it "is a curiosity in its way. It includes tea, sugar, lemons, soap, stay laces and a variety of articles, which could not be construed as stationery in any other but a Congressman's account. What Lowe can be doing with such large invoices of sugar and lemons, unless he runs a grocery or is partial to hot toddy and whiskey sour, we cannot conjecture. But we the reader must judge for himself from the account, as we find it published in the Kansas newspapers."

All these newspaper accounts show that Jerry Thomas's publisher was wise to add the whiskey sour to the third edition of his book.

## Variations and Iterations of the Whiskey Sour

By the late nineteenth century, the first variations of the whiskey sour were being developed.

### New York Sour

The oldest evolution is what is now known as the New York sour, which is made by simply pouring red wine over the back of a bar spoon into a whiskey sour. Although it's called a New York sour, it was invented by an anonymous bartender in Chicago, and its genesis is detailed in "A Barkeeper Tells a Reporter Some of the Secrets of His Art," which was first published in the *Chicago Tribune* and then went out on the news wire on December 4, 1883. The reporter recounts a conversation he had with a bartender named Tommy (no last name)—a man he calls "an artist." The reporter asks Tommy, "Is the whisky sour a popular drink?" He replies, "Well, our sours are very popular now. The claret 'snap' is what hits 'em hard. The claret makes the drink look well and it gives it a better taste. Men who drink our sours expect claret at every bar and when it is not put in they ask for it. It's getting circulated now, and other places are adopting our flourish."

In Charles A. Tuck's 1967 book *Cocktails and Mixed Drinks,* he called the addition of claret wine on top of a whiskey sour a "Continental Sour," which means that at some point the name had changed from the claret snap.

### Boston Sour, Egg Sour, and Other Eggy Cocktails

How egg whites came to be added to the whiskey sour, a variation sometimes called a Boston sour, is a bit confusing. Egg whites have a long history in cocktails, and many modern spirits writers state that the addition of egg whites to sours began at the close of the nineteenth century, but this is incorrect. Egg whites didn't appear in whiskey sours until Prohibition.

An online search for the history of egg whites in the whiskey sour leads to several accounts suggesting that they were first added to the cocktail in the late 1800s. Quite a few state that the first Boston sour recipe was published in William Schmidt's 1892 cocktail book *The Flowing*  *Bowl*. But if you actually read his book, you'll find no such cocktail. However, he did include the following whiskey sour recipe:

**Whiskey Sour**
A goblet with the juice of half a lemon or lime in the bottom,
a squirt of seltzer,
a little sugar; mix this.
⅔ full of ice,
a drink of whiskey; mix this well.

Strain, and serve.

There is also a drink called a whiskey daisy, with these instructions: "It is made as a whiskey sour; only put a dash of some cordial on top, such as chartreuse or curaçao." Another drink called the whiskey sour à la Guillaume appears as well:

**Whiskey Sour à la Guillaume**
A large glass with fine ice,

the juice of half a lemon,
3 dashes of gum,
a drink of whiskey,
2 spoonfuls of cream.

Shake this, strain, and serve.

Schmidt's book contains one recipe with whiskey, lemon, and egg called the Jack Frost whiskey sour, which may be what modern writers are referencing when they date the addition of egg whites, but the drink is nothing like an actual whiskey sour:

### Jack Frost Whiskey Sour
Into a mixing-glass squeeze the juice of half a
    lemon,
1 bar spoonful of sugar,
1 fresh egg,
1 pony of fresh cream,
1 drink of apple whiskey.

Fill your glass with cracked ice and shake thoroughly; strain into a high, thin glass, and fill the balance with imported seltzer.

Although whiskey sours didn't include eggs, plenty of other nineteenth-century cocktails did—both the yolks and the whites—and they were called flips. Eggs were also added to nogs, which often contained cream. A few specific cocktails such as the Tom and Jerry, which was sort of a hot nog, incorporated eggs as well. Jerry Thomas published such recipes in his book, but none of the sour recipes in any of the nineteenth-century editions included egg whites.

In fact, except for the use of egg whites in Thomas's—and Mrs. Beeton's—lemonade recipe, egg whites were not used in cocktails. Instead, Thomas and other cocktail writers of his era used egg whites to clarify syrups. *How to Mix Drinks* includes a whole section on making syrups, and Thomas discusses both the filtration and the clarification of syrups. "On the whole," he wrote, "*clarification*, is preferable for syrups to filtration. They need only be beaten up while *cold* with a little white of egg, and then heated; a scum rises which must be removed as soon as it becomes consistent and the skimming continued until the liquor becomes clear."

The first whiskey sours with egg whites weren't known as Boston sours, as they are today. They went by the more straightforward name egg sours. One memorable sour cocktail with egg whites was the Ramos gin fizz, first created in the late 1880s in New Orleans by Henry Ramos. It contained dry gin, powdered sugar, heavy cream, fresh lemon juice, fresh lime juice, an egg white, and orange flower water. Another was the Clover Club cocktail, believed to have been created at the Philadelphia gentlemen's club of the same name. It was made with an egg white, lemon juice, lime juice, Plymouth gin, sugar, and grenadine or raspberry syrup. Both these drinks contain gin, and it wasn't until the twentieth century that egg whites started to appear in recipes for sours made with whiskey.

Harry Craddock's monumental *The Savoy Cocktail Book*, published in 1930, instructed readers how to make a sour with the juice of half a lemon, a half tablespoon of sugar, and one glass of spirit "as fancy dictates." It was finished with a squirt of soda water and garnished with an orange and cherry. Craddock also included an egg sour recipe:

**Egg Sour**
1 teaspoonful of powdered white sugar
3 dashes of lemon juice
1 liqueur glass of Curacao
1 liqueur glass of Brandy
1 egg
2 or 3 small lumps of ice

Shake well and remove the ice before serving.

William Ferry's *Wet Drinks for Dry People,* published in 1932, also included egg white in a whiskey sour recipe. His instructions stated: "Shake all 3 items [2 ounces whiskey, 1 tablespoon lemon juice, and 1 teaspoon sugar] with ice. Strain and serve. A little egg white added before shaking enriches the drink, and I believe enhances the appearance."

Jean Robert Meyer wrote a book in 1934 called *Bottoms Up* that includes a recipe for a whiskey sour made with 1 jigger rye or scotch, 1 teaspoon gum syrup, and 4 dashes lemon juice. Alongside it is a recipe for a whiskey fizz that does not resemble earlier iterations of that drink and sounds a lot like a modern whiskey sour made with an egg white. It calls for 1 white of egg, 5 teaspoons lemon juice, 1 portion rye, 1 bottle soda water, and 1 teaspoon powdered sugar.

Some people surmise that, during Prohibition, bartenders used egg whites as one technique to soften and round out the rough edges of bad booze or bad moonshine. And sometimes, even after Prohibition, they continued to add egg whites to cocktails. But not every bartender or home mixologist added egg whites to their cocktails. Several advertorials in the 1930s and 1940s for Four Roses bourbon and Calvert Reserve, a New York blended whiskey, included recipes for whiskey sours consisting of only lemon, whiskey, and either granulated or powdered sugar. One 1937 advertisement for Calvert Reserve included instructions on how to make a "swell" whiskey sour with orange and cherry garnish, which is the most common whiskey sour garnish today.

## Mid-Twentieth-Century Whiskey Sours

By the 1950s, the egg white was well established as an ingredient in some versions of the whiskey sour. In *Bottoms Up*, Ted Saucier included a whiskey sour recipe from the Duquesne Club in Pittsburgh that was made with an egg white, 2 ounces rye, lemon juice, and granulated sugar.

In 1965 the *Bakersfield Californian* published a column by Philip Harding entitled "Enophile, the Cheerful Vintner," where he noted, "A Wisconsin reader has been researching the issue of getting a good head of foam on such potables as a Whiskey Sour." Harding shared the outcome with his readers: "J. L. Sanders reports good results with a secret ingredient—egg white. Simply make the drink in a blender with ice and other ingredients and add a small amount of egg white—at least ½ teaspoon per serving. It will have foam and a lovely body. I tried it. It didn't do much for my body. But foam? Hoo-boy."

In 1967 the *Fitchburg Sentinel* in Massachusetts published an advertorial titled "Sullivan's Package Store Offers Tips for Making Lively Drinks." It notes that "Paul Drapanos and Michael Kandianis, partners in Sullivan's Liquor Store at the Leghorn Rotary in Fitchburg, are experts in the easy-to-make-recipe department. Sullivan's work-saving tips tell you when to shake a drink or when to stir, how to chill glasses and which ingredient to put in first. For instance, the general rule for stirring is when the drink is made with clear liquors. Drinks that need shaking are made from fruit juices because they are harder to blend. For a frothy collar on drinks like a whiskey sour, add a tablespoon of egg white before shaking." These advertisements and articles explain the reasons for adding egg whites: body and froth.

The whiskey sour remained popular through the 1950s and 1960s. A bowling league in Wyoming Valley named its teams after drinks, including the Whiskey Sour, which "topped Gin Rickey in every game." And in 1960 there was a racehorse named Whiskey Sour that competed "in the big pony race in the Brentwood Running Horse Meet" in Tennessee. Whiskey Sour "won" two false starts plus the official race, meriting a photograph in the *Nashville Banner*.

Poppy Cannon wrote a syndicated column called "Ideas for Entertaining," and in 1963 she provided details on how to make "the smoothest sour." Cannon wrote: "A little orange juice mixed with the lemon juice makes a Whiskey Sour taste even better, cuts down on the amount of sugar needed. . . . To make a very special Sour for two: Use 2 tablespoons lemon juice; 1 tablespoon orange juice; 2 teaspoons superfine sugar and 4 ounces (½ cup) Walker's De Luxe Bourbon, aged eight years. Two or three dashes of aromatic bitters may be added. Hold the sugar entirely and you have what used to be called a Palmer."

In 1968 the *Colorado Springs Gazette-Telegraph* published an article about special treats to enliven the holiday season, including a recipe for a cranberry swizz that serves six: "Combine three cups of chilled cranberry juice cocktail, one-half cup whiskey sour mix, three-fourths cup whiskey and a beaten egg white. Shake until well blended and foamy. Season to taste with superfine sugar. If desired this may be shaken with one cup finely crushed ice and then strained when served. Serve very cold."

This cranberry swizz recipe incorporates an unfortunate trend of the 1960s: premade cocktail mixers. These mixers were all the rage and were heavily advertised in newspapers and magazines. Holland House sold bottled whiskey sour mixes so people could "serve perfect Whiskey Sours every time." Old Mr. Boston touted its packaged whiskey sour mixer by saying, "Now that you have the support, give the party." Mixers made serving cocktails easier, but they also made cocktails less tasty.

Just as mixers appeared on liquor store shelves for home consumption, bars also started using them. In the 1970s soda fountains were dying at pharmacies, so bars and restaurants installed soda machine systems and began to take shortcuts with whiskey sours, such as using soda guns and sour mixes containing artificial colors, artificial flavors, and preservatives. As famed mixologist and author Jeffrey Morgenthal wrote in a blog post, "Sour mix is a gateway drug. It can lead you down a very dark path, or it can open up a new world of fresh flavors or ingredients . . . let's face it: bland, weak, artificially-flavored sour mix is the vodka of non-alcoholic mixers. Add some raspberry to it, it tastes pretty much like raspberry. Add some whiskey and it's, uh, flavored whiskey. I guess."

Sour mixes, discos, and other fashionable trends of the 1970s led to what some people call the Dark Ages of the Cocktail. There were notable exceptions in places such as the French Quarter of New Orleans and the supper clubs of Wisconsin, which continued to turn out handcrafted cocktails. However, many bars and clubs stopped making cocktails with fresh juice. Sour mix—or, sometimes, sour soda—made it easy for bartenders to churn out drinks so customers could quickly get back on the dance floor. Bad whiskey sours made with sour mixes and soda guns continued into the 1980s, and they can still be found in dive bars everywhere. Thankfully, though, a curious and welcome revival of the classics started in the 1990s.

## The Whiskey Sour in 2000 and Beyond

By the early 2000s, a definitive cocktail revival was under way. Bartenders in big cities on both coasts were rediscovering the old classics, and in a series published in *Punch* in 2020, Robert Simonson described it best: "If there is one trend that epitomizes the whole of the cocktail renaissance, let alone its early years, it is fresh ingredients. During the '90s, the cocktail bar slowly converted itself from a supermarket aisle, filled with shelf-stable products rife with preservatives and chemicals, to a green grocer, where freshly plucked and sourced ingredients—juices, garnishes, eggs, everything—crowded the bar top every service."

Among the many cocktails bartenders rediscovered was the whiskey sour. Although it wasn't a standout in the early classic cocktail movement of the twenty-first century, it was on menus; more importantly, bartenders knew how to make it without using a soda gun. They took their inspiration from Jerry Thomas and other bartending authors of the late nineteenth century, squeezing fresh lemons for juice, but they switched out the straight sugar for simple syrups. The use of flavored simple syrups became common, and some bartenders occasionally substituted lime juice for the lemon juice.

No bar took the whiskey sour to modern heights like Milk & Honey in New York City. Opened by Sasha Petraske in 1999, Milk & Honey created not one but two distinctly modern twists on the whiskey sour. In 2000 Petraske's friend T. J. Siegal came to visit, and instead of having his bourbon sour made with simple syrup, he asked for the honey syrup being featured in a rum cocktail. That twist became the Gold Rush. In 2005 Milk & Honey added a new iconic drink, the Penicillin, which was created by Australian bartender Sam Ross. The Penicillin, which uses two types of scotch and a honey ginger syrup, is now arguably modern bartenders' favorite twist on the whiskey sour.

Ross crafted yet another modern iteration of the whiskey sour called the Paper Plane, which he invented for the Violet Hour in Chicago in 2008 at the request of another Milk & Honey alum, Toby Maloney. This cocktail became so beloved that there's even a craft cocktail bar in San Jose, California, named the Paper Plane.

Bartenders continue to riff on the whiskey sour, and it's likely that modern variations will continue to be added to the canon of classic drinks. Rescued from oblivion, the whiskey sour is here to stay. There's even a national Whiskey Sour Day, celebrated by whiskey marketers everywhere on August 29. Let's toast to that!

## Modern Pop Culture References

The whiskey sour is enjoying such popularity that it has been integrated into some modern books, movies, and television shows. Here are some examples:

1. In season four of *Mad Men,* Lane's father takes his son and Don to the Playboy Club. If you browse the vintage menus from locations around the globe, you'll find that this members-only club offered a lot of whiskey sours.
2. There are three books with the cocktail as a title:
   - J. A. Konrath's best-selling Lieutenant Jacqueline "Jack" Daniels mystery series starts with the aptly named *Whiskey Sour,* which came out in 2004.
   - Liliana Hart's *Whiskey Sour,* the second volume in her Addison Holmes mystery series, appeared in 2012. The series is about a history teacher who becomes a private investigator in Whiskey Bayou, Georgia.
   - Kim Loraine's *His Whiskey Sour,* a novella published in 2018, is part of The Cocktail Girls romance series set in Las Vegas. *His Whiskey Sour* is about a romance between a rock star and a cocktail waitress.
3. In 2019's *Once upon a Time . . . in Hollywood,* which is set in 1969, Rick Dalton, an aging actor played by Leonardo DiCaprio, slugs back numerous whiskey sours. In a particularly memorable scene, Dalton freaks out after flubbing his lines and berates himself by saying, "Eight [expletive] whiskey sours, I couldn't stop at three or four."
4. During the height of the COVID-19 pandemic, Ed Helms (of *The Office* fame) hosted an online variety show called "The Whiskey Sour Happy Hour" on his website, the Bluegrass Situation, which benefited the Music Cares relief fund.
5. A 2022 indie film by Christopher Selby titled *Whiskey Sour* was an official selection at the Phoenix Film Festival. The movie centers around old friends Cal and Joe, two middle-aged men who meet at a bar where old secrets

are revealed and they have to wrestle with lies and truths. The movie poster features a whiskey sour in a big rocks glass.

By the time you're reading this, there has probably been another whiskey sour reference in a television show, book, or film. David Wondrich once called the whiskey sour "the fried egg sandwich of American mixology," and as such, it never goes out of style.

# 2

# Formulas

The whiskey sour is a deceptively simple cocktail with only three ingredients—whiskey, lemon juice, and sugar—sometimes with a dash of bitters or an egg white. But at its heart, it's a three-ingredient cocktail. You can use better whiskeys, different sugars, or a variety of citrus juices, but the main element of a whiskey sour is the interplay of proportions.

In an interview for liquor.com by Amy Zavatto, Kenneth McCoy, a bartender at the now-closed Ward III cocktail bar in New York City, summed it up neatly: "It's one of those drinks that has a simple recipe, and therefore is easily [messed] up." McCoy is absolutely right—it's an easy cocktail to make, but it's just as easy to ruin. So how do you get it right?

## Perfecting Proportions

The first step is to know your own preferences, which sounds obvious but isn't. "Most people don't have any type of trained palate," says Daniel Beres, co-owner of the Lost Whale cocktail bar in Milwaukee and co-owner of Odyssea canned sangria. "If there's a spice blend in a drink, they can't pick out what it is, and they can only tell you whether they like it or not. As long as there are no off-putting flavors, they will enjoy the cocktail, but they can't tell you the reason why they like it." Ultimately, he says, "You need to learn yourself, learn what you like and dislike, and then you'll be able to go into a bar and order exactly what you want." That's especially true with a simple cocktail like the whiskey sour. To help you figure out which proportions best match your taste, this chapter examines some of the most popular variations.

In most recipes, whiskey sour ingredients are given in either parts or ounces. A part sounds like an imprecise measurement, but bartenders often use it because they make drinks to fit the glasses they're served in. Each part is basically an equal portion of the cocktail's total volume.

Parts can be converted into ounces or milliliters. Most recipes in this book list ingredients in ounces because most US bars use jiggers that hold 1 or 2 ounces. Then I met a bartender in Eau Claire, Wisconsin, who swears by milliliters. Joe O'Brien, who made me one of the best whiskey sours I've ever tasted, gave me his recipe in milliliters. "The reason for using milliliters is accuracy and speed," he says. "Even if you're using jiggers with the half- and quarter-ounce markings, it's not as quick as filling a jigger up to the top and dumping it into a cocktail shaker. Speed is everything."

No matter the unit of measurement, be sure to measure with care. Good bartenders use exact measurements because slight variations can make all the difference. It's hard to eyeball a quarter ounce, for example, and some of the most popular whiskey sour variations differ by only small amounts.

## The Formulas: Sour and Sweet

For the sake of conformity, in traditional whiskey sour recipes the sour refers to fresh lemon juice and the sweet refers to simple syrup, made of equal parts sugar and hot water:

**Simple Syrup**

1 cup hot water

1 cup sugar

Stir together until sugar is completely dissolved. Store in refrigerator for 1 to 2 weeks or freeze for up to 6 months.

Following are some formulas that use different proportions of sour and sweet.

### The Golden Formula Whiskey Sour

Two parts whiskey to ¾ part sour to ¾ part sweet is considered the golden formula for a whiskey sour. It is often served in craft cocktail bars and is the preferred formula for many whiskey connoisseurs.

This can be considered the Goldilocks of whiskey sours: it's not too sweet and it's not too tart; it's just right. "I do think that this is where you find the balance of whiskey without overpowering everything else," says Jason Van Auken, general manager and beverage director of Brandywine restaurant in Cedarburg, Wisconsin.

Balance is the key word here. "You get booze in the beginning, and then you taste the sweet and the sour, but there's still booze in the background and on the finish," Beres says. "It's always there throughout the cocktail. This is why it's the one for people who appreciate drinking a high-quality spirit neat or on the rocks."

This formula is my personal favorite, and it's the one most of my friends and family have swooned over. And when I present variations at cocktail-making classes, it is by far the most popular formula. However, it's not to everyone's liking. "In my mind, this is the [most] Zen balanced of the whiskey sours," says Brendan Cleary, bar manager at Great Lakes Distillery in Milwaukee. "But even though it's balanced, I don't think of it as a sour cocktail because you have equal parts sour to sweet. I think if you want a sour whiskey sour, you need more lemon juice."

### Golden Formula Whiskey Sour
2 oz. whiskey
¾ oz. fresh lemon juice
¾ oz. simple syrup
Glass: rocks or coupe
Garnish: orange or lemon slice and cherry

Place all ingredients in a cocktail shaker with ice. Shake for 30 to 60 seconds. Double-strain into rocks glass with ice or chilled coupe; add garnish.

### *The 2-1-1 or Balanced Whiskey Sour*
This formula—2 parts whiskey to 1 part sour to 1 part sweet—increases both the sour and sweet components while keeping the whiskey the same. This can translate to either 2 ounces whiskey, 1 ounce lemon juice, and 1 ounce simple syrup or 1½ ounces whiskey, ¾ ounce lemon juice, and ¾ ounce simple syrup. Either way, the whiskey's contribution is reduced. It's still a balanced cocktail, but it isn't a whiskey-forward whiskey sour. "In the 2-1-1, the booze lies more in the background of this

cocktail, and the booze doesn't hang on in the finish," Beres says.

The sweet and the sour hold equal weight in this cocktail—it's not so sour that your mouth puckers, and it's not so sweet that you're scraping sugar remnants from your teeth. It's still a balanced drink, but the whiskey taste is muted, making it a softer cocktail all around.

This wouldn't be the first choice of a seasoned whiskey drinker or a bourbon aficionado, but for those who tend to shy away from whiskey, it might be a good fit. "I'll dial down the whiskey," Van Auken says, "for a customer who usually doesn't drink whiskey." Beres notes, "If you're trying to introduce someone into the world of bourbon or whiskey, you're bringing down the amount of spirit to make it a bit less offensive, to give them the ability to enjoy a whiskey cocktail. There's still enough whiskey, yet it's not the complete star of the show."

### 2-1-1 or Balanced Whiskey Sour

2 oz. whiskey
1 oz. fresh lemon juice
1 oz. simple syrup
Glass: rocks or coupe
Garnish: orange or lemon slice and cherry

Place all ingredients in a cocktail shaker with ice. Shake for 30 to 60 seconds. Double-strain into rocks glass with ice or chilled coupe; add garnish.

### The Lemon Lovers' Whiskey Sour

For those who like sour, this formula might be their jam: 2 parts whiskey to 1 part sour to ¾ part sweet. "It's going to be more citrus-forward right from the mid-palate and into the finish," Beres says. "The whiskey will hit right away, but then it will dissipate, and the citrus takes over."

This is definitely the cocktail for people who prefer sour. The lemon jumps out and hits you in the beginning, middle, and end of a sip. The whiskey isn't quite as muted as in the 2-1-1, but it's definitely the wingman to the lemon juice.

Beres points out that this cocktail also appeals to people who are watching their sugar intake. "If someone asks me for no sugar, then as a bartender, I have to add something; otherwise it's too thin and unpalatable."

"This is the cocktail for someone who believes a sour has to be sour," Cleary says. "It's for a sour sucker."

#### Lemon Lovers' Whiskey Sour
2 oz. whiskey
1 oz. fresh lemon juice
¾ oz. simple syrup
Glass: rocks or coupe
Garnish: orange or lemon slice and cherry

Place all ingredients in a cocktail shaker with ice. Shake for 30 to 60 seconds. Double-strain into rocks glass with ice or chilled coupe, add garnish.

## The Less Whiskey, More Sour Whiskey Sour

This formula—1½ parts whiskey to 1 part sour to ¾ part sweet—is "for the same person who doesn't want sugar, but they also don't want too much whiskey," Beres says. The whiskey hides in the background, and even though there's more lemon juice than simple syrup, it's still pretty sweet.

**Less Whiskey, More Sour Whiskey Sour**
1½ oz. whiskey
1 oz. fresh lemon juice
¾ oz. simple syrup
Glass: rocks or coupe
Garnish: orange or lemon slice and cherry

Place all ingredients in a cocktail shaker with ice. Shake for 30 to 60 seconds. Double-strain into rocks glass with ice or chilled coupe; add garnish.

## The Mouth-Puckering Whiskey Sour

The whiskey sour gets progressively more sour when you dial back the sugar another quarter ounce: 2 parts whiskey to 1 part sour to ½ part sweet. "This is for someone who can really handle their citrus," Beres says. "Most people will need to take an antacid." And it's a good choice for those who don't want to consume much sugar.

"That's a real sour sour," Cleary says. Among the sour versions of the whiskey sour, the lemon juice is most prominent in this one, hitting the entire palate.

**Mouth-Puckering Whiskey Sour**
2 oz. whiskey
1 oz. fresh lemon juice

½ oz. simple syrup
Glass: rocks or coupe
Garnish: orange or lemon slice and cherry

Place all ingredients in a cocktail shaker with ice. Shake for 30 to 60 seconds. Double-strain into rocks glass with ice or chilled coupe; add garnish.

### The Whiskey Strong Yet Sour Whiskey Sour

This formula—2 parts whiskey to ¾ part sour to ½ part sweet—is heavy on the whiskey but still tart and fairly light on the sugar. Just dialing down the sour by a quarter ounce makes it a different cocktail. This one's for both whiskey and sour connoisseurs. "This is how I take my whiskey sours," says Jason Neu, founder and CEO of Soulboxer Cocktail, a bottled cocktail company that includes a whiskey sour in its lineup. "This is how I make my quintessential whiskey sour at home. I like it tart."

#### Whiskey Strong Yet Sour Whiskey Sour

2 oz. whiskey
¾ oz. fresh lemon juice
½ oz. simple syrup
Glass: rocks or coupe
Garnish: orange or lemon slice and cherry

Place all ingredients in a cocktail shaker with ice. Shake for 30 to 60 seconds. Double-strain into rocks glass with ice or chilled coupe; add garnish.

## *Mr. Boston's Old-School Whiskey Sour*

What makes this sour different from all the others is that instead of simple syrup it uses powdered sugar: 2 ounces whiskey, ½ ounce lemon juice, and ½ teaspoon powdered sugar. The powdered sugar contributes texture to the drink, not just sweetness. "It adds a silky mouthfeel," Beres says. "To me, this formula is for someone who wants to taste their bourbon or their whiskey and wants a bit of sweet and sour. The powdered sugar lops off the harsh corners of the citric acid from the lemon juice and a little bit of the alcohol burn from the booze itself. It's for someone who wants a more spirit-forward drink but something easier and lighter than their usual Manhattan or old-fashioned."

This is a delicious whiskey sour. When I've taste-tested it on friends and family, they've never found it too sweet or too sour, but it definitely tastes more boozy, even though it has the same amount of alcohol as some of the other recipes.

### Mr. Boston's Old-School Whiskey Sour
2 oz. whiskey
½ oz. fresh lemon juice
½ teaspoon powdered sugar
Glass: rocks or coupe
Garnish: orange or lemon slice and cherry

Place all ingredients in a cocktail shaker with ice. Shake for 30 to 60 seconds. Double-strain into rocks glass with ice or chilled coupe; add garnish.

### The Sweet Tooth Whiskey Sour

This variation is for people who have a real taste for sweetness: 2 parts whiskey to ½ part sour to 1 part sweet. It will make your teeth ache.

This recipe is from Tim Smith, third-generation moonshiner and star of the Discovery Channel's hit show *Moonshiners*. Tim's family has been making moonshine in the Appalachian Mountains for decades, and he now sells an aged version, Climax Woodfire whiskey, produced at a distillery in Virginia instead of in a pot still in the woods. The Smiths enjoy this sweet version of the whiskey sour, and Tim often adds egg whites for texture and an extra sprinkle of brown sugar on top of the orange and cherries.

**Tim Smith's Sweet Tooth Whiskey Sour**

2 oz. whiskey or Climax Woodfire whiskey
1 oz. simple syrup
½ oz. lemon juice
Glass: rocks or coupe
Garnish: orange or lemon slice
    and cherry

Place all ingredients in a cocktail shaker with ice. Shake for 30 to 60 seconds. Double-strain into rocks glass with ice or chilled coupe; add garnish.

### Testing Your Palate

If you really want to hone in on your own preferences, try making each of these versions of the whiskey sour and conducting a taste test. I've found that some people are good at predicting what they like, but most people don't know themselves as well as they think they do.

"Trying different versions will help you learn more about yourself, and at the end of the day, it's hard to go in and tell a bartender what you want or have them make you something if you don't know what you like or don't like and why," Beres says. "If you can figure out why you like or don't like something, that will help you in the future whenever you're trying new things." He believes there is a perfect whiskey sour for every cocktail lover. "If you like margaritas or other citrus cocktails, I'm sure you could find a whiskey sour recipe you'll dig."

If you're not up to the challenge of making every formula presented here, try making just the golden formula and the 2-1-1 or balanced whiskey sour. Compare them and see which one you prefer. If you prefer one over the other, but it's still not quite to your liking, start modifying your favorite by quarter-ounce increments. For example, if you prefer the golden formula but it's not quite sweet enough, add a quarter ounce of simple syrup. If it's not sour enough, add a quarter ounce of lemon juice.

When conducting taste tests, Beres recommends adding only a quarter ounce of one ingredient at a time. "You can always add, but you can never take away," he says. "That's a rule of thumb behind the bar." For example, if someone thinks Beres's standard whiskey sour—2 parts whiskey, ¾ part lemon juice, and ¾ part simple syrup—is too sour, he adds a quarter ounce of simple syrup and just rolls the drink back and forth between the shaker tins. "Usually, that's just enough for someone who wants it a bit sweeter," he says.

As illustrated by the formulas in this chapter, even slight variations can make a cocktail appealing or not.

Discovering exactly what you like about a drink will make you a more informed—and contented—consumer. "Once you know what type of whiskey sour you like or dislike, you can direct a bartender," Beres says. "You can go into a bar and say 'Hey, I know you use the 2-1-1 formula, but I like just a bit more lemon juice in mine' or 'I like it a little sweeter.' Then, as a bartender, I can rock one for you."

# 3

# Ingredients and Accoutrements to Create a Super Sour

The whiskey sour has only three main ingredients, yet there are endless ways to experiment with them and enhance your cocktail experience. This chapter takes a deep dive into the three basic components—whiskey, sour, and sweet—and examines how changing them slightly can transform your cocktail. Other less prominent components, such as bitters, egg whites, ice, and garnish, are covered too, as these seemingly minor details can improve and refine any whiskey sour.

## Whiskey and Other Spirits

Bourbon is probably the most popular whiskey to use in a whiskey sour. Its vanilla, caramel, and oaky notes meld well with the sourness of lemon and the sweetness of sugar, making it the standard choice in many bars. Other options include scotch, rye, American single malt, Japanese whisky, Irish whiskey, and Canadian whisky, each of which imparts a slightly different flavor to the cocktail.

If you like spice, rye whiskey is a great choice. Rye adds a kick of flavor, and a whiskey sour made with rye has more bite and sharpness than a traditional bourbon-based sour. Kira Webster, beverage director for Indo and

Nippon Tei in St. Louis, says, "I prefer rye whiskey. It's robust, and the spices come through really nicely."

For a smokier taste, try scotch or American single malt. A scotch sour is smooth, with undertones of peat and a definite smoky aroma. It tastes almost heavy. American single malts can make an even smokier yet smooth cocktail, with more oomph than a typical whiskey sour.

Irish whiskey lends a smooth, mellow taste to the sour, while Japanese whisky makes a fragrant, soft, and more nuanced sour. Canadian whiskies, especially aged ones, result in a smooth yet intense whiskey sour. Tennessee whiskeys add a sweet aroma and a bit of spice.

A whiskey sour made with white or unaged whiskey or moonshine will have a slightly different taste than a traditional whiskey sour, given the absence of oak or caramel notes. It is more akin to a daiquiri or gimlet in taste and mouthfeel.

The type of whiskey you use is not nearly as important as its quality. In general, a decent bottle of whiskey can be had for $20 to $30, and some great ones can be purchased for a bit more or less. If you already have a favorite whiskey on hand, my advice is to use it. You can also do an online search and read reviews of whiskeys, or you can look into the products being offered by local craft distilleries. More and more craft distilleries are opening, and some of them make fantastic whiskeys, but others are overpriced. Just because a whiskey is handcrafted or made in small batches doesn't mean it's better than spirits made by larger companies. And just because the distillery's tasting room manager is enthusiastic about a whiskey doesn't mean you have to love it too. Let your taste buds be your guide.

Be sure to check the whiskey's proof. A whiskey that's 80 or 86 proof is a lot less potent than one that's 100 or 105 proof. Daniel Beres notes that when using a higher-proof whiskey, a little extra sugar may be needed, especially if the whiskey sour is made with egg white. Sugar helps round the edges of a higher-proof whiskey.

You can also blend different whiskeys together—called "splitting the base"—which can be quite delicious. Diane Corcoran, Michigan sales director for Traverse City Whiskey Co., says, "I love mixing our rye with our apple whiskey." Some bartenders use a combination of bourbon and rye to mute the rye's spiciness and add honey to the flavors of the bourbon. This is how Jason Van Auken makes a whiskey sour. "I'll use a heavier bourbon and a little rye to add spice," he says.

You can also split the base between whiskey and some other type of spirit. Rum is a particularly decadent choice, especially if it was aged in bourbon or whiskey barrels. "I'll combine a high rye with a rum," Van Auken says. "A split base allows you to layer flavors of the cocktail. It's a lot of fun." Brandy and cognac add an interesting note, especially if you're going to float some wine on top and make a New York sour. These spirits are distilled from grapes, and they really bring out the wine's aroma. Aged gins, mezcals, and tequilas all play well with whiskey too. Unaged gins and even vodkas can also work.

You can substitute a liqueur for some of the whiskey in a whiskey sour, or you can simply add the liqueur to the recipe, turning the sour cocktail into what is called a daisy cocktail. Fruit and nut liqueurs work particularly well as accents for a whiskey sour, and some coffee liqueurs add a nice touch. Any liqueur can be used except for a cream-based liqueur, as the lemon juice will make it curdle.

You can also change the cocktail by infusing the whiskey with tea, fruit, or nuts. Chapter 4 includes some recipes for infusions.

## Simple Syrup and Other Sweet Bases

The earliest whiskey sour recipes called for granulated sugar, powdered sugar, or sugar cubes, but most modern whiskey sour recipes call for simple syrups.

A basic simple syrup is made with equal parts granulated sugar and hot water, such as 1 cup sugar and 1 cup hot water (although some recipes call for 2 parts sugar to 1 part water). Unless otherwise specified, the simple syrups included in the recipes in this book use the 1:1 ratio. Some cocktail nerds actually weigh the water and sugar to make sure they are exactly equal, and others measure the sweetness in their cocktails using refractometers. Although this is techy and fun, it's not necessary. You don't have to do anything fancy with the water either. You don't even have to boil it. Hot tap water is fine, as long as your tap water tastes good, or you can just heat the water in a microwave.

Most important is making sure that all the sugar has dissolved. You don't want gritty sugar granules floating in the syrup. It's also important to cool the syrup to room temperature before using it, especially if you're adding egg white to the cocktail. If the syrup is too hot, it might actually cook the egg white, which is not a tasty experience.

Any granulated sugar will do for a basic simple syrup recipe. It

can be hard to discern a taste difference between organic sugar harvested from lovingly tended sugarcanes and generic store-bought granulated sugar. You can, however, vary the whiskey sour by using different sugars and sweeteners. Turbinado sugar, brown sugar, maple syrup, and honey all provide a distinct twist.

Turbinado sugar, made from the first pressing of the sugarcane, adds a caramel-like sweetness and more depth of flavor than plain white sugar. Demerara sugar, which has some molasses in it, is similar. Demerara and turbinado sugar can be used almost interchangeably. Brown sugar also contains molasses. Any of these sugars will bring out the whiskey's caramel, oak, and vanilla notes. I like using a dark sugar if I'm making a spiced syrup with cinnamon, nutmeg, cloves, or ginger. Dark sugars are also a good choice if you want to add apple cider to your cocktail, and they pair amazingly well with fruity peach or apple whiskeys.

Maple syrup also brings out the vanilla and caramel notes of whiskey. Honey adds brightness and a floral note—especially if you use a floral honey. That's how the modern classic the Gold Rush came into being. Agave can also be used in place of simple syrup. It works especially well if you're splitting the whiskey base with an agave-based spirit like tequila or mezcal.

Just as you can split the whiskey base, you can also split the sugar base. For example, you can use half regular simple syrup and half maple syrup in your whiskey sour.

Flavored simple syrups are another easy way to elevate a whiskey sour. You can use spices, herbs, fruits, or citrus peels to infuse simple syrups and create an entirely different cocktail profile. Chapter 4 features recipes for a variety of simple syrups.

You can also purchase ready-made simple syrups, which are available at liquor stores and online. There are dozens of different flavored syrups, some of which are specifically designed for cocktails. You can also use flavored syrups meant for coffee drinks.

Simple syrups should be stored in the refrigerator, where they'll stay fresh for up to two weeks. Alternatively, you can freeze them for up to six months.

### Citrus Juices

The main caveat here is to use fresh juice. Forget the bottled, shelf-stable stuff. If you use anything but fresh, your cocktail will suffer—you might as well add sweetened vinegar to your drink. "It's all about the freshest juice. Always avoid the bottle if you can," says Fitz Bailey, brand ambassador and mixologist for Brown-Forman Distillery in Louisville, Kentucky. "If you can get that fresh, fresh juice, that's where the money's at."

Fresh lemon juice is the gold standard for whiskey sours, but you can also use lime juice, as the two have similar amounts of sugar. Mixing juices—such as blending equal parts lemon and lime juice—can add dimension to a cocktail. "One of the best markers for quality is complexity," says Amanda Beckwith, lead blender and education manager for Virginia Distilling Company in Lovingston, Virginia. "By mixing, you can add layers and add depth. That's why I gravitate toward the lemon-lime combo again and again." Whenever Beckwith makes juleps, for example, she always adds a little bit of lime juice. "I was inspired by mojitos, and I've found it makes them zippier and more complex," she says. Bailey is also a fan of the lemon-lime combination, and so is Ina Garten, the Barefoot Contessa. She uses a split juice base whenever she makes a whiskey sour. Using both fresh lemon and lime juice results in a delightful, delicious, and more complex version of the whiskey sour. Simply mix equal parts lemon and lime juice, then measure out the amount needed for the cocktail.

You can also use other citrus juices, such as orange and grapefruit, or other fruit juices, such as apple. But you should still add some lemon or lime juice for the sour portion of the cocktail. If you use only orange juice, for example, there won't be enough sour to create a balanced cocktail. Chapter 6 is devoted to the art of mixing it up with different juices.

When working with fresh juices, make sure that any seeds and bits of fruit have been removed. That's why bartenders often double-strain cocktails before serving.

Ideally, fresh juice should be used immediately. Most bartenders recommend using it within a day of squeezing. It can last up to three days in the refrigerator, or it can be frozen for up to a year.

If you're too lazy to squeeze the juice yourself, Cheeky, Twisted Alchemy, and Fresh Victor all sell fresh juices (Fresh Victor combines the juice with sweeteners). Perfect Purée from Napa Valley also offers some amazing fruit purées. Its strawberry, hibiscus, blood orange, and yuzu purées all go really well with sour cocktails.

Hand squeezers often work better than automatic juice machines. With some of these appliances, the juice takes on a bitter or metallic aftertaste because of how the pith and peel are removed.

If you want to take it a step further, you can clarify the fresh juice. "What I like about clarifying is that it only removes, it doesn't add anything," Bailey says. Clarifying removes the color and any leftover pulp, but it doesn't affect the fresh flavor. To clarify juice, use agar-agar, a vegan product made from seaweed. "It's a white powder, and Amazon has it in a big jar, and if you buy it, it will last forever," Bailey says. For juices such as lemon, lime, or pineapple, use 1.3 grams of agar-agar per 100 milliliters of juice. (To clarify a non-citrus juice like strawberry, use 0.9 gram of agar-agar per 100 milliliters of juice.) Whisk the agar-agar into the juice, bring it to a boil over medium heat, and pour the mixture into a bowl over an ice bath (a bigger bowl of water containing ice). Let it set for 10 to 15 minutes, or until the texture resembles gelatin. Pour the gelatin-like curds into a strainer lined with cheesecloth and press down on it until the juice runs clear. "You will have this completely clear juice that is really gorgeous," Bailey says. "What you're left with is the flavor, and it's a lighter beverage. There's almost a pure feeling about drinking it."

To create a slightly different juice profile, grill the citrus before squeezing it. This adds a touch of smoke. You can also smoke lemons and other fruits in a smoker. Drew Kassner, general manager of The Cheel in Thiens-ville, Wisconsin, recommends grilling the citrus halves before adding them to the smoker to get a smokier result.

### Bitters

Bitters make everything better. Bitters are botanicals—fruits, barks, peels, and the like—infused into a neutral spirit. Bitters both tie the cocktail's components together and bring out their different elements, making the sum of the cocktail greater than its parts. "Bitters almost behave like salt does in cooking," Ross Salchow says. "You won't necessarily taste them, but they'll bring out all the flavors of the drink."

Usually one to three dashes of bitters is enough for a single cocktail. With the whiskey sour, you need to decide when to add the bitters: before shaking the cocktail or as a final dash on top. This depends on whether you're adding egg white. "If you're using egg white, always put the bitters on top," Bailey says. This adds a pop of color to the top of a foamy sour. But even if you don't add egg white, Jason Neu recommends putting the bitters on top to intensify the cocktail's pleasant aroma with that first sip.

To make the drink more visually appealing, apply the bitters to the top of the cocktail with a dropper. For a creative design, place three or more drops in a row and then drag a toothpick through the middle of them to make a ring of hearts.

Angostura bitters are the gold standard in a whiskey sour, and they are the bitters of choice for many bartenders. They are the most widely available brand of aromatic bitters, and they boast a bright red color. If you compare a whiskey sour made with Angostura bitters against one made with another brand of aromatic bitters, you'll notice some subtle fragrance and taste differences, but you can use any aromatic bitters in a whiskey sour. They all add depth and brightness.

But aromatic bitters aren't the only choice. Orange bitters, Peychaud's bitters, coffee bitters, walnut bitters, and other types of bitters accentuate different elements and aromas in a whiskey sour cocktail. Corcoran is a big fan of experimenting with bitters. "I've done citrus,

Peychaud's, chocolate bitters, and more," she says. "Hellfire bitters give a nice little bit of heat. Cherry bitters and plum bitters are fun. It depends on the season and on my mood." Van Auken prefers Peychaud's bitters, but he sometimes uses Orleans bitters, made by Scrappy's. "It's a little more anise, and it lends a little bit of a different profile," he says. "It can be overpowering, but if you're using a higher-proof bourbon or rye, it works well. A whiskey sour is a very approachable cocktail, and a little bitters can really change it up." Other great bitters to try are black walnut bitters (Fee Brothers), cherry bark vanilla bitters (Bittercube), and Aztec chocolate bitters (Fee Brothers). "But no one should ever put down Angostura bitters," says Salchow, "it's the all in all bitters."

Orange or other citrus bitters bring out the lemon aroma, making it stronger and more pronounced. A whiskey sour made with Angostura or aromatic bitters has a hint of cinnamon and clove, while one crafted with orange bitters smells more citrusy. Black walnut, pecan, and other nut bitters add a nutty aroma, and chocolate bitters add a chocolatey note. Peychaud's bitters provides a red brightness (slightly different from Angostura's hue) and a bit of anise. Cherry bitters accentuate the cherry garnish, and vanilla bitters bring out the whiskey's oak and vanilla notes.

Just as you can use a combination of whiskeys and juices in a whiskey sour, you can mix two different kinds of bitters. Orange and Angostura, for example, play well together and add complexity. Other options are orange and pecan, orange and walnut, or Angostura and cherry bitters.

If you feel really adventurous, you can make your own bitters, using recipes found in old-time cocktail books and online. A lot of the ingredients can be found at specialty spice shops, but most bitters recipes call for some unusual ingredients. For example, gentian root, which is used to add bitterness to bitters, is available online from Dandelion Botanical Company. A bitters maker called Bitters Club sells not only bitters but also spice blends to make homemade bitters.

Tinctures are another interesting and easy-to-make addition to sour cocktails. They are basically one-note bitters. Combine the flavor of your choice—cinnamon, lavender, lime, or whatever—with high-proof grain alcohol and let it marinate for a week to a month, until the aroma is to your liking. Chapter 4 provides a basic recipe for tinctures.

## Egg Whites and Alternatives

Not all whiskey sours are made with egg whites, but those that are can be pretty spectacular. Egg whites add a velvety texture and mouthfeel to a cocktail. "Egg white is kind of magical," says Liz Henry, co-owner of J. Henry & Sons Bourbon in Dane, Wisconsin. "Just like we like things that have bubbles, we like egg white because it adds that texture and richness. Egg whites not only elevate the cocktail; they elevate the whole cocktail experience."

If you use really fresh egg whites or pasteurized egg whites, your cocktail will be foamy and luxurious without an eggy taste. But, as Van Auken notes, "People sometimes get a little spooked by egg whites." If you have concerns about using raw eggs, buy eggs from a local farmer that you trust. Simply crack the egg white into the cocktail shaker and discard the yolk. If you're not a big fan of wasting the yolks, refrigerate them and use them for a fresh hollandaise sauce. You can also use pasteurized egg whites, which are sold by the quart in many grocery stores. Just pour the egg whites from the carton right into a cocktail jigger.

If you're vegan or allergic to eggs, other products are available to add foam and texture to sour cocktails. Aquafaba is probably the number-one egg white alternative. Aquafaba is chickpea water—the foamy liquid at the bottom of a can of chickpeas. It's amazing in cocktails, and just like egg whites won't make a cocktail taste eggy, aquafaba won't make a cocktail taste like chickpeas. A lot of bars have switched to aquafaba so that everyone can enjoy the same velvety cocktail. Paul Sutton Bourbon founder Myra Barginear prefers to use aquafaba in her perfect whiskey sour.

Technically, any liquid from cooked beans is considered aquafaba, but the liquid from red beans or black beans isn't clear like an egg white, so chickpeas have become the default aquafaba bean. You can make aquafaba by cooking chickpeas from scratch or buy a powdered version of it, called Vör Faba Foamer, online. Vör is rather expensive, though; a 7-ounce jar will set you back about $40.

Another option is Fee Brothers Fee Foam, but this isn't aquafaba. It's a chemical foamer for cocktails and includes ingredients such as propylene glycol and polysorbate 80. Some reviewers found that it added a chemical aftertaste to their cocktails.

Another foamer on the market is Ms. Better's Bitters Miraculous Foamer. It's pricey, at $30 to $35 per 4-ounce bottle, but an entire bottle of this vegan foamer is the equivalent of about 100 egg whites. This is what Van Auken uses, and it "really does the trick," he says. Just add three or four drops to the cocktail, dry-shake, then add ice. It creates a beautiful foam on top, and although

> ### Dry Shake versus Wet Shake versus Reverse Shake
>
> When making a cocktail that contains egg whites or cream, most bartenders first do a dry shake—that is, they agitate the ingredients without ice to break apart the egg whites or the cream. Then they add ice and shake again. The objective is to create better foam. If you just throw all the ingredients into the shaker with ice and then shake and strain, the foam won't be as voluptuous.
>
> Some bartenders shake the egg white alone and then add the other cocktail ingredients for a dry shake. Another technique is to shake all the ingredients except the egg white with ice, remove the ice, then add the egg white and shake again. This is called the reverse shake. This technique, while more labor intensive, creates the most voluminous amount of foam—the closest you can get to a merengue on top. This is especially desirable when serving a whiskey sour in a coupe or martini glass. But if you're serving the cocktail in a rocks glass filled with ice, it's not as visually impressive.

it's not quite the same mouthfeel as aquafaba, it's good enough, according to Van Auken.

## Garnish

Garnish may be the most overlooked part of a cocktail, especially when making drinks at home. Many people use great whiskey and fresh juice but then either forget the garnish entirely or use mass-produced maraschino cherries.

The typical garnish for a whiskey sour is what bartenders call a flag—a cherry sandwiched between a folded orange slice on a skewer (this can be a metal or plastic skewer or a wooden toothpick). Alternatively, sours can be garnished with a cherry wrapped in a long slice of orange peel and then skewered. You can vary the orange portion of the garnish by using fresh blood oranges or Cara Cara oranges, which are more colorful, or you can use dried orange wheels, which add a dramatic and sophisticated touch.

Perhaps the most overlooked part of the garnish is the cherry. Rather than using cheap, artificially colored cherries, an easy way to up your game is to use better cherries. Luxardo cherries, imported from Italy, are a fantastic option. These candied cherries are soaked in a thick Marascara cherry syrup made without any thickening agents or preservatives. They also tend to be the most expensive cherry on the market, costing upward of $20 a jar.

Amarena cherries are another good option. They're also made in Italy, and they can sometimes be found in stores like Trader Joe's. They're not as expensive as Luxardo, but some versions contain gluten, so be sure to read the label if you're gluten-sensitive.

There are also some great cherries produced state-side. Traverse City Whiskey Co. makes locally sourced whiskey-soaked cherries. (Traverse City, Michigan, is considered the cherry capital of the world.) Like Luxardo, they're viscous and delicious, and because they're made with whiskey, they're perfect for a whiskey sour. They cost about $15 a jar and can be shipped anywhere (although they are made with booze, they are *not* booze).

Another boozy cherry option comes from a craft distillery in Wisconsin. Central Standard Distillery uses Door County cherries soaked in its own brandy. They're boozy and more viscous than maraschinos, and they're less expensive than Luxardo cherries.

Seaquist Orchards in Door County, Wisconsin, also makes a cocktail cherry using locally grown cherries that are an upgrade from maraschinos. Although they're not nearly as viscous as Traverse City or Central Standard cocktail cherries and are not infused with booze, at $5 per jar, they're a tasty bargain.

Woodford Reserve makes bourbon-soaked cherries, but depending on where you buy them, they can be as expensive as Luxardo cherries. The Filthy brand makes Filthy black cherries—Italian Amarena cherries soaked in a thick sauce—and they're less expensive than Luxardo. These are stellar options for upping your garnish game.

Most of these premium cherries come at a premium cost—$10 or more for a 10-ounce jar. But if you're a do-it-yourself kind of person, you can make your own premium cherries at a lower cost. When Door County cherries are in season and I can find them at my local farmers' market, that's what I do. But if locally grown cherries aren't an option, you can use any good fresh or frozen cherries. There's a recipe for Whiskey Cherries in chapter 4.

Fresh citrus also makes a great garnish for a whiskey sour. A wheel of lemon, a wedge of grapefruit, or a peel of lime makes a visually dramatic garnish. Dehydrated citrus wheels are also visually appealing.

When using a fresh citrus peel as garnish, squeeze it to express the oils and add an aromatic pop to the cocktail. For an even bigger burst of flavor, Jane Danger, mixologist for Pernod Ricard, recommends putting a lemon peel in the shaker with the other ingredients. "Just throw the peel in the cocktail tin before you shake," she says. The lemon oils expressed by shaking intensify the lemon flavor. You can also add an orange peel—even if you're not using orange juice in the sour. If the whiskey has orange notes, adding a peel during shaking brings out those notes, Danger says.

## A Pinch of Salt

Salt isn't just for margaritas. It can enhance a whiskey sour too.

I had never considered adding salt to a whiskey sour until my friend Ellen took me to a speakeasy in Indianapolis. She drove us to a building in the Broad Ripple neighborhood; we entered through the side door, wandered down a corridor past some dentists' offices and whatnot, and heard some muffled music behind a plain door. We sat at the bar, and I ordered a whiskey sour, taking note of all the steps as the bartender crafted it. He cracked a farm-fresh egg for the egg white and used the magic proportions of 2 ounces whiskey, ¾ ounce simple syrup, and ¾ ounce lemon juice, plus bitters. Then he dribbled a couple drops of something into the cocktail. When I asked, he told me it was saline. The result was sublime. It was a whiskey sour, but it was creamy and smooth and one of the best whiskey sours of my life. And the only difference from what I was making at home was the salt.

"Saline is such an underutilized ingredient," says Neu. "It helps round things out, and it makes flavors work better together. It's also good to use if you taste something imbalanced or clunky about a cocktail, like if you're trying to pull out one flavor, and you get too much of another."

So, of course, I had to re-create this magical sour at home. After researching the proper saline solutions for cocktails, I learned that the ideal ratio is 4 parts water to 1 part salt. The bartender in Indianapolis recommended using sea salt, but you can use any high-quality salt without any iodine added.

### Saline Solution
4 tablespoons boiling water
1 tablespoon sea salt

Whisk salt into boiling water until completely dissolved. Makes ¼ cup.

This recipe makes enough saline solution for about 600 cocktails. A quarter of a cup contains nearly 1,200 drops of water, and you need only 2 drops to wake up the flavors in a whiskey sour. Any more will likely ruin the drink. It won't necessarily taste salty, but it will taste bitter and might make you gag. "The two things that are most difficult to add to a cocktail are salt and orange flower water," Salchow says. In both cases, it's easy to add too much, and in terms of flavor, less is more.

Unlike a margarita, you don't want to taste the salt when you sip a sour. Just 2 drops wakes up the palate; it enhances the tartness of the lemon juice, the sweetness of the sugar, and the bitterness of the bitters. But it doesn't taste like you added any salt. If you do a side-by-side taste test—one whiskey sour with saline and one without—you'll notice the difference. The one without the saline tastes good, but not quite *as* good as the one with saline.

To ensure that you add only 2 drops, I recommend using a dropper. Any dropper from a used bitters bottle or a medicine dropper from the local pharmacy will do. If you tend to be heavy handed, you might want to drop the saline onto a spoon before spilling it into the cocktail shaker.

If you don't want to go to the trouble of making a saline solution, Neu says you can add barely a pinch of fine kosher salt or sea salt to a cocktail—but again, err on the side of caution. It's better to add too little than too much. Just as a five-star chef uses salt to enhance the flavors of her dish, a smart bartender uses just a touch of salt to flavor cocktails.

## Ice

The last ingredient in a whiskey sour—if it's being served in a rocks glass—is ice. If you've ever noticed that the ice at certain bars and restaurants is much cooler, clearer, and prettier than normal ice, you're absolutely right. "Ice really does matter," Beckwith says. Those crystal-clear ice cubes, large or small, are supplied to bars and restaurants by companies that specialize in making these high-end ice cubes. The cubes themselves are clear, and they look like glass melting into the drink. The ice is frozen solid, without air pockets, which means that the cubes dilute the drink more slowly. And they're usually made from special water without fluoride or any other chemicals that could affect the taste.

The average consumer may find it hard to obtain these ice cubes. Large or midsized cities usually have companies that sell specialty ice to bars, restaurants, and sometimes liquor stores. When sold direct to consumers, this ice can be pricey, as a dozen small cubes can cost $10 or more. The good news is that you can make it yourself.

Beckwith advises starting with good water. "It makes a difference because as ice melts, it will dilute your cocktail, and you will taste it," she says. Van Auken recommends using a 12-quart Igloo cooler, but any brand will do. "The main thing is that it has to be insulated," he says. Fill the cooler three-quarters full of water. It's important to use a clean cooler and a clean freezer that contains no other items, as they will impart flavor to the ice. Leaving the top off, put the cooler in a deep freezer for 24 to 30 hours. The water will freeze from the top down, pushing any impurities to the bottom of the cooler. "Directional freezing is the way to go," Van Auken says. Remove the large block of ice, chip off the bottom, and then carve and chisel the ice into smaller cubes for cocktails. Van Auken recommends a 2-inch by 1-inch cube for whiskey sours. "This creates a beautiful, precision-cut ice cube, and hand-carved ice is a nice touch to a cocktail," he says.

If you don't have a freezer big enough to fit a cooler inside, another option is to use fancy ice cube trays. You can even add herbs or citrus peels to the water before freezing to give your drinks a pop of color. Van Auken infuses butterfly pea flower tea into water, then adds a sprig of thyme to each cube. The water freezes into a beautiful blue color; then, when the ice cube encounters citrus, it turns purple.

"Ice can add another visual element to your drink," Beckwith says. "If you use smaller ice cubes, it will create a more slushy experience, but if you use big ice cubes, it will not water down your drink very quickly." Danger says, "You can have fun with ice, and there are a lot of different silicone molds for ice, like roses, and you can put rose petals in the ice cubes." Besides petals, herbs, fruits, or vegetables like cucumbers, you can add edible glitter to ice cubes. Edible glitter for baking comes in misters or in sprinkle form. According to Danger, you can freeze half cubes, add a layer of glitter, top with water, and freeze again. Alternatively, you can swirl the glitter into the ice. "The glitter can stay suspended or mixed throughout," she says.

## The Glass

Whiskey sour cocktails are typically served in one of three glasses: a rocks or old-fashioned glass, a coupe or martini glass, or a highball or Collins glass. Collins glasses are typically taller and narrower than highball glasses, but most casual drinkers won't notice the difference.

Coupe and martini glasses are great for presentation. When serving whiskey sours without ice, the stems of these glasses keep your hands from warming the cocktail too quickly. When serving whiskey sours with ice, a rocks glass is typically used.

Generally speaking, a narrow glass intensifies the drink's aromas, whereas a glass with a wide mouth allows the cocktail to breathe and mellow a bit. Of the three styles of glasses used for sours, the coupe and martini glasses tend to make the cocktail most aromatic, followed by highball or Collins glasses, and last, rocks or old-fashioned glasses. That said, the rocks glass is probably most popular when serving a whiskey sour.

When it comes to glasses, size matters. A standard whiskey sour recipe fits nicely into a standard-sized coupe, rocks, or martini glass, but if you use a highball or Collins glass, you'll have to add more ice or more cocktail to fill the glass to the rim. Similarly, if you use your granny's small antique cocktail glasses, they'll be overflowing with only half a standard recipe. Conversely, if you use an oversize martini or double rocks glass, you'll need to double the recipe to fill it to the top.

The optimal glass type can also depend on the ingredients. If you're using fresh egg white in your cocktail, Bailey cautions against serving it in a coupe or martini glass. "The space on top in those glasses sometimes allows some of the sulfur elements of the egg white to become more noticeable," he says. "A huge, wide mouth on a coupe makes the drink not as pleasant as it could be. Not every egg's going to have that problem, but I try to eliminate that possibility if I can." If you really want to serve a frothy sour in that type of glass, Bailey recommends using either pasteurized egg white or aquafaba.

It's also important to note that whenever you're serving a cocktail without ice, the glass should be chilled. To chill glasses, either place them in a freezer or add ice and water to the glass, let it sit for 30 to 60 seconds, drain, and then pour the cocktail in. A chilled glass keeps the cocktail cold for a longer period of time and makes the drinking of it more enjoyable.

## Putting It All Together

Now that you've got the parts of the cocktail figured out, it's time to put them together to create the ultimate whiskey sour cocktail. This recipe uses the golden formula (see chapter 2), but the proportions can be changed to suit your personal preferences.

**The Ultimate Whiskey Sour**

2 oz. whiskey

¾ oz. fresh lemon juice and lime juice mixture

¾ oz. simple syrup

1 egg white or ½ oz. pasteurized egg white or
   egg white substitute

2 drops saline solution

2 or 3 drops or dashes Angostura bitters or other
   bitters

Glass: rocks or coupe

Garnish: orange slice and high-quality cherry

Place all ingredients in a shaker, except for
the bitters. Shake for 30 to 60 seconds, add
ice, and shake for another 30 to 60 seconds.
Double-strain into rocks glass with ice or chilled
coupe, carefully drop bitters on top, and then
add garnish.

# 4

# Syrups, Infusions, and Other Enhancements

This chapter is all about experimenting in the kitchen or behind your home bar. "There are all these things you can do, little modifications to make your sour really special," says Jane Danger. There are many ways to modify and personalize a whiskey sour or even take it in a whole new direction. Here, you'll find techniques and ideas to elevate the whiskey sour and make it even more decadent and special.

## Simple Syrups and Beyond

As the name suggests, simple syrup is simple to make. Flavored syrups are almost as easy, although they take a little more time because they're infused with fruits, spices, herbs, and other ingredients. They're great to use in any whiskey sour, but some recipes call for certain syrups.

All these syrups can be stored in the refrigerator for up to a week, but unless you're having a party, you're not likely to use up a batch of simple syrup within that time. If that's the case, you can pour the leftover syrup into glass bottles or plastic bags, label and date them, and put them in the freezer. Then, if you get a hankering for a rhubarb whiskey sour or a blackberry smash, you can just take the syrup you need out of the freezer. Since the cocktails are shaken with ice, you don't even need to thaw the syrup. Simply use a spoon to measure out the right amount of syrup slush and add it to the cocktail shaker.

### Honey Syrup
1 cup hot water
1 cup honey

Whisk until the honey is completely dissolved.

### Rich Honey Syrup
½ cup hot water
1 cup honey

Whisk until the honey is completely dissolved.

### Maple Syrup
1 cup hot water
1 cup maple syrup

Whisk until the maple syrup is completely dissolved.

### Rich Demerara Syrup
2½ cups demerara sugar
1 cup very hot water

Whisk until the sugar is dissolved.

## *Fruit Syrups*
Fruit syrups add a fruity touch to a regular whiskey sour. However, they do *not* go well with any type of whiskey smash. A blackberry-sage smash, for example, tastes great with plain simple syrup and even better with sage simple syrup, but blackberry syrup would make the drink too sweet when muddled fruit is added to the mix.

After making fruit syrups, you'll be left with the discarded fruit solids. They taste like fresh jam, albeit with more seeds than regular jam, and can be used as a fresh fruit spread on toast or over ice cream. You can also mix the leftover fruit solids with equal parts unsweetened applesauce and create fruit leather if you have a dehydrator.

If you don't want to go to the trouble of making a fruit-based simple syrup, you can use jam to achieve a similar profile. Orange marmalade, strawberry jam, and raspberry jam, among others, all add a pop of color and flavor. The basic rule of thumb is to add 1 bar spoon of jam to the whiskey sour recipe of your choice.

**Blueberry Syrup**

1 cup blueberries
1 cup sugar
½ cup hot water

In a medium-sized bowl, mash blueberries and sugar together. Cover and let sit for at least 2 hours or up to 4 hours at room temperature. Pour in hot water and stir. Let the mixture sit until cooled, about 20 minutes. Strain through a fine-mesh sieve or cheesecloth. Makes about 1½ cups syrup.

**Raspberry Syrup**

1 cup raspberries
1 cup sugar
½ cup hot water

In a medium-sized bowl, mash raspberries and sugar together. Cover and let sit for at least 2 hours or up to 4 hours at room temperature.

Pour in hot water and stir. Let the mixture sit until cooled, about 20 minutes. Strain through a fine-mesh sieve or cheesecloth. Makes about 1½ cups syrup.

**Blackberry Syrup**
1 cup blackberries
1 cup sugar
½ cup hot water

In a medium-sized bowl, mash blackberries and sugar together. Cover and let sit for at least 2 hours or up to 4 hours at room temperature. Pour in hot water and stir. Let the mixture sit until cooled, about 20 minutes. Strain through a fine-mesh sieve or cheesecloth. Makes about 1½ cups syrup.

**Strawberry Syrup**
1 cup strawberries
1 cup sugar
½ cup hot water

In a medium-sized bowl, mash strawberries and sugar together. Cover and let sit for at least 2 hours or up to 4 hours at room temperature. Pour in hot water and stir. Let the mixture sit until cooled, about 20 minutes. Strain through a fine-mesh sieve or cheesecloth. Makes about 1½ cups syrup.

## Rhubarb Syrup

When your rhubarb plants are growing like crazy and you're sick of baking, make a syrup and add some tart red deliciousness to your cocktails.

1 cup sliced rhubarb
1 cup sugar
1 cup water

Place all ingredients in a small pot and cook over high heat, stirring until the sugar is dissolved. Bring to a boil. Reduce heat and simmer for 20 to 30 minutes. Remove from heat and cool completely. Use a slotted spoon to remove rhubarb pieces. Makes about 1½ cups syrup.

Note: If you have a dehydrator, you can dehydrate the rhubarb pieces and use them as cocktail garnish or fruity snacks (see the recipe later in this chapter).

## Peach Syrup

This syrup is great when combined with a peach whiskey like Old Camp.

1 cup peeled, sliced peaches
1 cup sugar
1 cup water

Place all ingredients in a small pot and cook over high heat, stirring until the sugar is dissolved. Bring to a boil. Reduce heat and simmer for 20 to 30 minutes. Remove from heat and mash the peaches. Cool completely and strain, pressing down to get all the juice. Makes about 1½ cups syrup.

## Lemon Cordial

For an intense lemon flavor, give a lemon cordial a try. To serve with whiskey, stir together 1 part cordial, 2 parts whiskey, and 1 part soda water.

1 cup water
1 cup sugar
1 cup fresh lemon juice (from about 8 lemons)
Zest from 8 lemons

Place water and sugar in a medium-sized saucepan over medium-high heat and bring to a boil. Whisk in lemon juice and lemon zest and reduce heat to medium, stirring frequently until thickened. Remove from heat and cool completely. Press through a sieve. Can be stored in the refrigerator for up to a week or frozen for up to 6 months.

Note: For greater depth and viscosity, add an ounce of vodka or moonshine.

## Oleo Saccharum Syrup

This just sings with flavor and tastes amazing in any whiskey sour recipe.

Peels from 8 lemons
Peels from 4 oranges
Peels from 4 limes
2 cups granulated sugar
1 cup hot water

Place peels and sugar in a bowl, cover, and let sit for 24 hours at room temperature. (The oil from the peels combines with the sugar to create a slushy mixture that's part liquid and part slurry.) Add hot water, stir, and strain. Makes 2¼ cups syrup.

Note: Traditionally, when making any variety of oleo saccharum, the citrus oil and sugar mixture is just strained, without adding water. The leftover peels can be made into candied citrus peels and used as garnish (see the recipe later in this chapter).

### Lemon Oleo Saccharum Syrup

Peels from 9 to 10 lemons
1 cup granulated sugar
½ cup hot water

Place peels and sugar in a bowl, cover, and let sit for 24 hours at room temperature. Add hot water, stir, and strain. Makes 2¼ cups syrup.

## Herb and Spice Syrups

### Cinnamon Simple Syrup
*Upstream Brewing Company, Omaha, Nebraska*

4 cups water
4 cups sugar
4 to 6 cinnamon sticks

Place all ingredients in a medium-sized saucepan. Bring to a boil over high heat. Remove from heat and cool completely, 1 to 2 hours. Remove cinnamon sticks. Refrigerate for up to a week or freeze for up to 6 months.

### Basic Herbal Simple Syrup

This syrup can be made with any fresh herbs—mint, sage, thyme, tarragon, basil. You name it, you can use it. Herbal syrups add a layer of complexity without overwhelming the cocktail. They also pair well with smash recipes. Basil syrup is great in a strawberry smash, for example.

1 cup sugar
1 cup water
1 bunch (about ¼ cup) fresh herbs

Place sugar and water in a small saucepan over medium heat. Bring to a simmer, add herbs, stir, and turn off heat. Cover and let sit at room temperature for at least 2 hours or up to 12 hours. Strain. Refrigerate for up to a week or freeze for up to 6 months.

### Lavender Simple Syrup

1 cup sugar
1 cup water
2 tablespoons dried lavender buds

Place sugar and water in a small saucepan over medium heat. Bring to a simmer, add lavender buds, stir, and turn off heat. Cover and let sit at room temperature for at least 2 hours or up to 12 hours. Strain. Refrigerate for up to a week or freeze for up to 6 months.

### Rosemary Syrup

*Pat McQuillan, cofounder, Central Standard Distillery, Milwaukee, Wisconsin*

McQuillan created this simple syrup to use in a cocktail with smashed blackberries (see the Standard Sour in chapter 7).

1 cup water
1 cup sugar
4 sprigs rosemary

In a small saucepan, combine water and sugar. Cook over medium heat until sugar dissolves, but do not boil. Add rosemary and simmer for 10 minutes. Remove from heat, cool, and strain. Makes about 2 cups syrup.

**Cinnamon, Sage, and Cranberry Syrup**
*Amanda Beckwith, lead blender and education manager, Virginia Distillery Co., Lovingston, Virginia*
This is the perfect syrup for a holiday-centric whiskey sour.

1 cup fresh cranberries
1 cup water
1 cup sugar
4 cinnamon sticks
10 fresh sage leaves

Place all ingredients in a medium saucepan and bring to a boil. Reduce to a simmer and cook, stirring occasionally, until the cranberries burst open and achieve a fairly smooth consistency when stirred—about 10 minutes. Remove from heat and strain, pressing the solids with a spoon to release the juice. Cool and then refrigerate for up to 3 weeks.

Note: To make a cranberry simple syrup, just omit the cinnamon and sage.

**Sugar Snap Pea and Cilantro Syrup**
For a garden-fresh cocktail, this is the syrup you'll want to use. Any herbs fresh from the garden can be substituted for the cilantro in this versatile recipe.

1 cup water
1 cup granulated sugar
1½ cups sugar snap peas, roughly chopped
1 handful (about ½ cup) fresh cilantro leaves

Place water and sugar in a small saucepan and bring to a boil. Stir in sugar snap peas and cilantro and remove from heat. Let sit for at least 30 minutes. Strain. Store for up to a week in the refrigerator or freeze for up to 6 months.

**Strawberry-Thyme Syrup**
Strawberries go well with just about any herb, but thyme is a particularly refreshing one. You can substitute basil, rosemary, sage, or whatever herb tickles your taste buds.

1 cup strawberries
1 cup sugar
20 sprigs fresh thyme
½ cup hot water

In a medium-sized bowl, mash strawberries and sugar together. Stir in thyme. Cover and let sit for at least 2 hours or up to 4 hours at room temperature. Pour in hot water and stir. Let sit until cooled, about 20 minutes. Strain through a fine-mesh sieve or cheesecloth. Makes about 1½ cups syrup.

### Vanilla Syrup
*Kira Webster, beverage director, Indo and Nippon Tei, St. Louis, Missouri*
This syrup enhances the vanilla aromas of a whiskey.

4 cups simple syrup
1¾ teaspoon vanilla extract

Whisk both ingredients together.

### Honey-Ginger Syrup
Honey and ginger are a classic pairing. This is the syrup used in the Penicillin.

1 cup honey
1 cup water
4-inch piece ginger, peeled and roughly chopped

Place all ingredients in a small saucepan over high heat. Bring to a boil, reduce heat to low, and simmer for 5 minutes. Cool and strain. Refrigerate for up to a week or freeze for up to 6 months.

Note: For ginger syrup, leave out the honey. You can use demerara or turbinado sugar to make another rich syrup.

### Spiced Orange Syrup

This syrup is particularly good in recipes with either apple cider or orange liqueur.

1 cup water
1 cup sugar
Zest from 1 orange
2 cinnamon sticks
2 star anise
3 or 4 cardamom pods

Place all ingredients in a small saucepan on medium-high heat and bring to a simmer. Simmer for 5 minutes. Cool completely and strain. Makes about 1 cup.

Note: You can use brown sugar or turbinado sugar and add an orange pekoe tea bag to the mix.

### Easy Ginger Beer Ginger Syrup

If you don't want to peel and chop fresh ginger, this is an easy substitute for ginger syrup.

2½ cups ginger beer (made with real sugar)

Put ginger beer in a small saucepan over high heat. Bring to a boil, reduce heat to low, and simmer until reduced to ½ cup.

### Rich Aromatic Syrup

This syrup is great for fall cocktails and pairs well with apples, peaches, and pears.

1 cup hot water
2 cups turbinado sugar
3 cinnamon sticks

3 whole star anise
3 whole cardamom pods

Mix ingredients together until sugar is dissolved. Let spices infuse for at least 20 minutes or up to 24 hours.

Note: To make a pumpkin spice variation, replace the cardamom and star anise with ½ teaspoon whole cloves; 1 inch peeled, roughly chopped fresh ginger root; and ⅛ teaspoon freshly grated nutmeg.

## Tea and Other Assorted Syrups

### Sweet Tea Simple Syrup
*Wolf Moon Bourbon, Lawrenceburg, Indiana*

1 bag black tea
1 cup hot water
1 cup sugar

Steep tea according to directions. Stir in sugar until dissolved.

Note: Make other tea syrups using Earl Grey, green tea, oolong tea, white tea, and even chai tea. All of them make delicious simple syrups.

### Hibiscus Simple Syrup
This lovely syrup adds a bright red color to cocktails. For garnish, use dried, candied hibiscus flowers, which you can buy online or at some grocery stores.

1 cup sugar
1 cup water

1 hibiscus tea bag or 1 tablespoon loose-leaf
hibiscus flowers

Bring water to a boil. Add tea and sugar and stir until sugar is dissolved. Turn burner off. Let tea steep for at least 5 minutes or up to 2 hours.

Note: For a brighter red color, use 2 tea bags or up to 2 tablespoons loose-leaf hibiscus flowers.

### Butterfly Pea Tea Syrup

If you want to shake up a dramatic cocktail, use this syrup. Butterfly pea tea is a deep blue color when brewed, but when you add acid—lemon juice—it changes into a lovely purple hue. Mix up your sour cocktail with everything but the lemon juice, then pour it on top and watch the color magically change.

1 cup water
2 tablespoons butterfly pea tea
1 cup sugar

Heat water to almost a boil, or about 190 degrees Fahrenheit. Add tea and sugar and stir until sugar is dissolved. Remove from heat and steep for at least 10 to 15 minutes. Strain.

### Homemade Grenadine

1 cup pomegranate juice
1 cup sugar
1 teaspoon orange blossom water
¼ teaspoon vanilla extract

Place pomegranate juice and sugar in a small pot over medium-high heat and stir until sugar is dissolved. Reduce heat to low and simmer for 5 minutes. Remove from heat, cool, and then stir in orange blossom water and vanilla extract. Refrigerate for a week or freeze for up to 6 months.

### Orgeat

This almond-based syrup is used for tiki drinks, but it can also be added to whiskey sours, especially when modified with Amaretto.

1 cup unsweetened, high-quality almond milk
1 cup granulated sugar
⅛ teaspoon orange blossom water
⅛ teaspoon almond extract
⅛ teaspoon vanilla extract

Place almond milk and sugar in a small pot and bring to a boil over medium-high heat. Reduce heat to low and simmer for 10 minutes. Cool for at least 20 minutes. Add orange blossom water, almond extract, and vanilla extract. Makes 1¼ cups. Refrigerate for a week or freeze for up to a month.

### Great Lakes Super-Secret House Sour Mix

*Brendan Cleary, bar manager, Great Lakes Distillery, Milwaukee, Wisconsin*

"This is meant to be used with your favorite Great Lakes whiskey," Cleary says. It's a rich sour mix that can be used in place of both juice and syrup in cocktails.

5 oz. fresh lemon juice
5 oz. fresh lime juice

4 oz. agave syrup
2 oz. Good Land cranberry liqueur
2 oz. Sprecher cream soda
1 oz. Good Land orange liqueur
20 dashes grapefruit bitters
10 dashes Angostura bitters

Mix all ingredients together. To make an equal-parts cocktail, combine 2 oz. whiskey with 2 oz. sour mix. Otherwise, combine the ounces of juice and simple syrup to determine how much sour mix to use. This recipe yields enough to make 10 cocktails.

### Candy Syrups

You can turn any type of sour or sugary candy into a simple syrup. Nick Nagele, cofounder of Whiskey Acres in DeKalb, Illinois, uses Lemonheads, but you can try it with Sour Patch Kids, gummy bears, Skittles, Starburst, lollipops, or any other hard or chewy candy.

#### Lemonheads Syrup
*Nick Nagele, cofounder, Whiskey Acres, DeKalb, Illinois*

1 cup Lemonheads or other sour candy
½ cup water
2 tablespoons sugar

Place Lemonheads in a small saucepan, cover with water, and heat on high. After 3 to 4 minutes, stir with a wooden spoon to break the candies apart. After 8 to 10 minutes, the lemon oil and sugar dissolve, and the candy centers form a viscous, gloopy mass. Strain the liquid out and stir the sugar into the liquid. Discard the solid mass. Makes 1 cup syrup.

## Infusions

Infusing whiskey with herbs, spices, and fruits gives cocktails an added dimension and an extra layer of flavor. Some infusions—tea, for example—can be made quickly in just 30 minutes to 2 hours. Others take days, weeks, or months. The longer the infusion time the greater the flavor. It's important to use a nonreactive vessel, such as a glass mason jar. You can also buy expensive infusing devices online.

Infused whiskey makes a fantastic gift, especially if you put it in a fancy bottle. I reuse those heavy green bottles that gourmet balsamic vinegars and olive oils come in. If you're feeling ambitious, you can create a whiskey sour gift basket or gift bag by adding some dried lemon wheels, simple syrup, and lemon juice.

### Tea Infusions

For tea infusions, the basic proportion is 1 to 2 tablespoons loose-leaf tea to 1 cup whiskey. Combine the two in a nonreactive glass jar or bowl and let it sit for anywhere from 30 minutes to 2 hours—more time equals more flavor. In addition to basic black tea, try green teas, oolong teas, flavored teas such as Earl Grey, and chai teas.

"I'm addicted to tea," Beckwith says. She uses different teas in different seasons to both infuse whiskey directly and make tea syrups.

### Fruit Infusions

You can infuse whiskey with whole fruit or just the peels. Oranges work great with most whiskeys, bananas (some bartenders recommend adding the peel) pair well with scotch, and exotic fruits like lychees work with Japanese whiskies. It's fun to play around with different flavors.

The usual ratio is 1 cup fruit to 1 cup whiskey, and the process is simple: Place the whiskey and fruit in a mason jar, seal it, store it somewhere out of the light, and smell and taste it after a day. If you like it, it's ready. If it's not strong enough, let it go another day and taste it again. For most people's taste, the infused whiskey will be ready in 3 to 7 days.

The one exception, for me, is cranberry-infused whiskey. When I was working on my first cocktail book, *Drink Like a Woman*, I had the opportunity to interview Joy Perrine, who was aptly known as the bad girl of bourbon. She taught me the proper way to make a mint julep and a mint simple syrup, as well as how to infuse mint into bourbon. "My grandmother was a madame and a bootlegger, and my father was a rum runner," she told me. Booze and bourbon were in her blood, but she didn't get into bartending until she moved to the Virgin Islands. In 1978 she relocated to Kentucky and spent the next twenty-five years tending bar and telling stories at the Equus Restaurant and Jack's Lounge. Sadly, Perrine passed away in 2019, but this is her technique for infusing cranberries into whiskey. This recipe never made it into *Drink Like a Woman*, but it's absolutely the whiskey you'll want to use for Thanksgiving, Christmas, Chanukah, and New Year's Eve whiskey sours.

### Cranberry Infusion
1 cup fresh cranberries
1 cup bourbon or other whiskey

Place cranberries and bourbon in a nonreactive jar, such as a mason jar. Cover and let it sit for 1 month. Shake once a week. Strain cranberries out and reserve for some other use, such as the sugarcoated cranberries described later in this chapter.

It really takes a whole month to make cranberry-infused whiskey. For the longest time, it just looks like a bunch of cranberries sitting in a jar of whiskey. But eventually, the whiskey takes on a lovely bright red hue, and the tart cranberry flavor seeps into the whiskey.

### Herb and Spice Infusions

When making infusions, whole spices and fresh herbs work better than the ground versions. For example, if you want to infuse whiskey with cinnamon, use whole cinnamon sticks; for a sage infusion, use fresh sage leaves. The basic recipe is a handful of whole spices—anywhere from ¼ to 1 cup—or a handful of whole herbs—anywhere from ¼ to ½ cup. The more you add, the more quickly the flavor will infuse. Try cardamom, star anise, whole vanilla beans, mint, or rosemary—all these flavors work well with whiskey. Most herb and spice infusions take anywhere from a day to a week.

### Nut Infusions

Pecans are a natural choice for a whiskey infusion, especially bourbon. But you can also use almonds, pistachios, or whatever nuts you go nuts for.

The ratio is ½ to 1 cup roughly chopped nuts to 1 cup whiskey. The process takes 3 to 7 days.

### Infusions with Bacon, Cheese, and Other Fatty Things

You can infuse whiskey with bacon, blue cheese, butter, cacao, or chocolate. The same basic rules apply, but for a bacon infusion, once you've achieved the desired flavor, put the jar in the freezer and, once it's frozen, skim the fat off the top.

## Garnishes

If you have fresh cherries, you can make your own whiskey cherries. (Frozen cherries can be used, but fresh are much better.)

### Whiskey Cherries

¼ cup water

¼ cup turbinado or demerara sugar or Sugar in the Raw

2 dashes Angostura bitters or other cocktail bitters

½ teaspoon vanilla extract

2 wide strips lemon peel (optional)

1 lb. pitted fresh cherries

1 cup whiskey

In a small saucepan over medium-high heat, whisk together water, sugar, bitters, and vanilla extract until the sugar is completely dissolved. Add lemon peels and bring to a boil. Add half the cherries and boil for 5 minutes. Remove from heat and stir in the remaining cherries and whiskey. Cool completely and pour into a nonreactive container such as a mason jar. Refrigerate, covered, for at least a day before using. Store in the refrigerator, covered, for up to 6 months.

**Sugarcoated Cranberries**
*Amanda Beckwith, lead blender and education manager, Virginia Distilling Co., Lovingston, Virginia*
This dramatic garnish is perfect for late fall and winter cocktails.

1½ cups sugar, divided
½ cup water
8 oz. package fresh cranberries

Combine ½ cup sugar and water in a medium saucepan. Bring to a boil over medium-high heat. Cool for 15 to 20 minutes, then stir in cranberries, mixing until they're thoroughly coated. Place cranberries in a gallon-sized container or bag, pour the remaining 1 cup sugar on top, seal the container, and shake to thoroughly coat cranberries with sugar. Spread cranberries on a baking sheet and place in the refrigerator for 20 to 30 minutes to let the sugar harden and the berries cool completely.

There's a movement in bartending to create less waste, and one of the easiest ways is to use dehydrated citrus wheels as garnishes for drinks. You can buy them, but they cost $5 to $15 for a 3-ounce bag. You can sometimes find dehydrated lemons, sweetened dried orange slices, candied mandarin orange slices, dried mango slices, and dried mango slices dipped in chili powder at Trader Joe's, and these work well as garnishes for whiskey sours. Dehydrated cherries can also be used, but they're not as good as upscale cocktail cherries. Another option is dehydrated cranberries, but they're tiny and can create a pulpy mess in the drink.

What I like about the dehydrated option is that dried citrus wheels travel well, and oranges or sweetened lemons become almost like a chewy piece of candy at the bottom of the glass. They're also quite easy to make if you have a dehydrator at home.

### Dehydrated Citrus Wheels

1 lb. fresh citrus fruit—lemons, limes, oranges, or grapefruits

Scrub the outside of the fruit to remove any wax, and use a paring knife or a mandolin to cut into ¼-inch-thick slices. Set the dehydrator to 130 to 140 degrees Fahrenheit. Arrange the wheels evenly on the dehydrator trays, leaving space in between them. Dehydrate for about 24 hours. The wheels become brittle when completely dried. Makes about 1½ cups dehydrated fruit. Store in an airtight container for up to 1 year.

### Candied Citrus Wheels

1 cup hot water
1¼ cup sugar, divided
1 lb. fresh citrus wheels—lemons, limes, oranges, or grapefruits

Whisk together water and 1 cup sugar. Set aside. Scrub the outside of the fruit to remove any wax, and use a paring knife or a mandolin to cut into ¼-inch-thick slices. Set the dehydrator to 130 to 140 degrees Fahrenheit. Dip fruit slices in sugar water and arrange them evenly on the dehydrator trays, leaving space in between them. Sprinkle slices with the remaining sugar. Dehydrate for about 24 hours. The wheels become brittle when completely dried. Makes about 1½ cups dehydrated fruit. Store in an airtight container for up to 1 year.

### Dehydrated Rhubarb
Leftover rhubarb pieces from rhubarb syrup

Set dehydrator to 130 to 140 degrees Fahrenheit. Arrange rhubarb pieces evenly on the dehydrator trays, leaving space in between them. Dehydrate for about 10 hours. The rhubarb will be chewy, like fruit leather, when done.

### Candied Citrus Peels
Leftover citrus peels from oleo saccharum syrup

Set dehydrator to 130 to 140 degrees Fahrenheit. Arrange the peels evenly on the dehydrator trays, leaving space in between them. Dehydrate for about 5 hours. The peels will be brittle when done. Makes 1 to 2 cups.

Edible flowers make beautiful, visually interesting garnishes and add a sophisticated touch to cocktails. Other garnish options include dried flowers, such as lavender buds or edible rose petals, and candied flowers, such as candied hibiscus flowers.

## Tinctures

Tinctures are basically one-note bitters. A lavender tincture, for example, is just lavender-infused high-proof alcohol, usually vodka or brandy. But if you're making a tincture to use in whiskey sours, you can use a high-proof whiskey. Besides lavender, cinnamon, fresh ginger, star anise, cardamom, and other baking spices go very nicely in a whiskey sour. You can make tinctures with citrus peels, too.

As a basic guideline, use about ½ cup dried ingredient and 1½ to 2 cups high-proof alcohol. To make a lavender tincture, for example, cover ½ cup dried lavender with 2 cups high-proof vodka and let it sit for about a month, shaking every few days.

## Fancy Rims

Adding sugar or spices to the rims of glasses is one way to enhance your cocktail presentation. It looks elegant and adds sweetness or spiciness to every sip.

To sugar the rims of cocktail glasses, you'll need a wedge or two of lemon or lime, a small shallow plate (a saucer works nicely), and sugar. Pour 2 tablespoons granulated sugar into the saucer. Take the citrus wedge and slide it around the rim of the glass. Then dip or delicately twirl the rim in the sugar.

If you want to get even fancier, you can use colored pastry sugars, Sugar in the Raw, demerara or turbinado sugar, or regular brown sugar. Granulated maple sugar or honey crystals work too.

For a spicy sour or a Whiskeyrita (see chapter 5), dip the rims in a combination of sugar and sea salt or kosher salt. You can also use smoked paprika, ground chilies, or a Mexican seasoning blend like Tajin.

## Misting

For a bit of aromatic panache, bartenders often squeeze the citrus peel right on top of the drink to give it a beautiful hint of lemon or orange. To take it to the next level, you can try misting a little bit of liquid on top of the drink. For instance, instead of doing a float of orange liqueur, put it in an atomizer and spritz it on top.

"When I think about making cocktails, I think about baking or making ice cream," Danger says. "With ice cream, because it's so cold, you can't always smell it. With cocktails, it's the same, so I like to add a bit of aromatics—some mint or basil or a mist of something." To emphasize the smoky nature of scotch cocktails, Danger says, "I'll mist a little bit of mezcal on top to bring out the smoke, especially for a winter cocktail."

A misting of orange blossom water brings out the citrusy elements in a whiskey sour. Rose water can also be misted. The effect of misting a whiskey sour, according to Danger, is akin to adding a float of peach brandy to a julep. "A mist on top can help balance a cocktail," she says. It also adds a bit of flair and is a nice finishing touch before serving a cocktail.

# 5

# Classic Riffs

The whiskey sour has spawned more riffs that have become classic cocktails in their own right than any other whiskey cocktail. This makes sense because spirits, citrus, and sugar provide a strong base for experiments resulting in delicious new creations.

Some of these classic cocktails date back to the 1800s, while others came of age in the early 1900s. Prohibition spawned several new twists on the whiskey sour, as the addition of fruit and sugar goes a long way in covering up the taste of bad whiskey and making it more palatable. But the most recent riffs are modern classics developed during the latest cocktail revolution in the twenty-first century. I have no doubt that bartenders will continue to create new classics to add to the canon of great cocktails.

## Cherry Bounce

Cherry bounce started out in the eighteenth century as a cordial or a spirit infused with fruit, spices, and sweeteners. It was popular during colonial times, and George Washington was reportedly fond of it. The spirit of choice for the cherry bounce was either brandy or whiskey.

One of the most entertaining stories about this drink originated in Chattanooga, Tennessee, in 1904. A man by the name of J. D. Allen was on trial, facing four charges of illicit trafficking in intoxicating liquors. He was accused of "using hypnotic Power on one Witness to Get

Him to Testify to the Effects of 'Cherry Bounce.'" The witness had apparently tasted the cherry bounce and found it "intoxicating." (This was a bad thing?)

Even though the cherry bounce technically predates the whiskey sour, it can be considered a riff because it is basically a whiskey daisy or a whiskey sour that has been modified with cherry liqueur. Here are two versions of the cherry bounce:

### Cherry Bounce Cordial

4 cups cherries, with or without pits
750 mL whiskey
3 to 4 cups sugar

Poke each cherry with a fork or knife so the whiskey can saturate it. (If the cherries are pitted, skip this step.) Place sugar and whiskey in two large jars with well-fitting lids and shake until most of the sugar is dissolved. Divide the cherries between the two jars and replace the lids. Let them sit for a week in a sunny spot, shaking them once or twice a day. Then store the jars in a cupboard or pantry for 1 to 2 months. When you're ready to drink the cordial, strain the liquid and set the cherries aside for use in pies or over ice cream (or, to use them in cocktails, put them in small glass jars and cover with more whiskey).

Variation: To make a more traditional cherry bounce, add a couple of cinnamon sticks, some cloves, and some star anise to each jar, along with the zest of 1 or 2 lemons.

**Cherry Bounce Cocktail**

1½ oz. bourbon or other whiskey
½ oz. cherry liqueur or cherry bounce cordial
½ oz. lemon juice
½ oz. simple syrup
2 dashes Angostura bitters
Glass: highball
Garnish: fresh cherry

Place all the ingredients in a shaker filled with ice and shake for 30 seconds. Strain into a highball glass filled with ice and garnish with a cherry.

Note: Every cherry liqueur is a bit different, depending on what kind of cherries it's made from (maraschino, Luxardo, and so forth). Cherry Heering is a Danish liqueur, and some fantastic liqueurs are made by craft distilleries in the United States. For instance, Great Lakes Distillery in Milwaukee makes a local cherry liqueur called Good Land Door County cherry liqueur (if you're familiar with *Wayne's World*, you'll get the joke).

## Whiskey Collins or John Collins

Back in the 1800s, the Collins was a popular style of drink made with liquor, lemon, and sugar and topped with soda water. The Tom Collins was made with Old Tom gin, and the John Collins was made with London dry gin, but in the modern era, the John Collins was sometimes made with whiskey instead of gin. In any case, this classic cocktail is basically a cross between a whiskey sour and a whiskey highball.

2 oz. whiskey
¾ oz. lemon juice
¾ oz. simple syrup
3 to 4 oz. club soda
Glass: highball or Collins
Garnish: lemon wheel, wedge, or twist

Place whiskey, lemon juice, and simple syrup in a cocktail shaker filled with ice and shake for 60 seconds. Strain into a glass, top with club soda, stir gently, and garnish with lemon.

## Whiskey Buck (aka Whiskey Mule)

Back in the nineteenth century, long before Moscow mules were popular, bucks were simple highballs made with ginger beer or ginger ale and lime juice. Today, this classic cocktail goes by several other names: whiskey mule, Kentucky mule (if made with Kentucky bourbon), or Tennessee mule (if made with Tennessee whiskey).

1½ oz. whiskey
½ oz. lime juice
4 to 5 oz. ginger beer or
  ginger ale
Glass: copper mug or highball
Garnish: lime wedge

Add ice to a shaker, pour in whiskey and lime juice, and stir for 60 seconds. Fill a copper mug or a highball glass with ice, strain the whiskey and lime juice into it, top with ginger beer, and garnish with a lime wedge.

## Rock and Rye

Back in the nineteenth or perhaps even the eighteenth century, this cocktail masqueraded as a cure-all, and it was served and sold in both pharmacies and saloons. Today, you can buy it ready-made in a bottle (Hochstadter's Slow & Low Rock and Rye is one brand) or you can make your own. It's basically rye whiskey infused with citrus, bitters, and rock candy. Sometimes dried fruit or something more exotic, such as star anise or horehound, is added. Harry Craddock included a simple recipe for Rock and Rye in his 1930 book *The Savoy Cocktail*. It was made with rye whiskey, dissolved rock candy, and "the juice of 1 lemon . . . if desired." Here's an updated version of his recipe:

2 oz. rye
½ oz. lemon juice
¾ oz. rich demerara syrup (see recipe in
    chapter 4) or prepared cane syrup
1 dash Angostura bitters
Glass: rocks
Garnish: rock candy

Place all the ingredients in a shaker filled with ice and shake vigorously for 60 seconds. Strain into a glass filled with ice and garnish with rock candy.

Note: You can buy prepared cane syrup online. Made from sugarcane juice, it's thicker than corn syrup and not as cloying. You can also make cane syrup from scratch, but it's a bit complicated and requires a candy thermometer and patience. If you're game, you can find recipes online.

## The Ward 8

This cocktail was named in honor of a beloved Boston politician: Martin Lomasney. Lomasney, the son of Irish immigrants, worked his way up in city politics, serving as alderman, state representative, and state senator. However, he was most well known for being the boss of Ward 8, on the city's West End. It is believed that the drink was created at the Locke-Ober French restaurant in 1898 to celebrate Lomasney's election to the state legislature.

2 oz. rye
¾ oz. lemon juice
¾ oz. orange juice
2 teaspoons grenadine
2 dashes Angostura bitters and/or orange bitters
Glass: rocks or coupe
Garnish: orange wheel and cherry

Place all the ingredients in a shaker filled with ice and shake for 60 seconds. Strain into a rocks glass filled with ice or a coupe glass. Add garnish.

## Hawaii Cocktail (or Klondike)

This cocktail originated in Hawaii in the late 1800s. A similar—or identical—cocktail called the Klondike originated around the same time in Alaska. The original recipes for both cocktails called for the "juice of one orange," and they were both stirred in the glass without bitters. The modern interpretation calls for a more exact measurement of orange juice, shaking rather than stirring, and the addition of bitters, since bitters make everything better.

1½ oz. whiskey, preferably bourbon or rye
1½ oz. orange juice
2 dashes orange bitters
Ginger ale
Glass: Collins
Garnish: peel of 1 orange

Pour whiskey, orange juice, and bitters into a shaker filled with ice. Shake for 60 seconds. Line a Collins glass with the orange peel, add ice, and strain the cocktail into the glass. Top with ginger ale.

## The Prince of Wales

This Victorian-era cocktail was named after Prince Albert Edward, known as Bertie to his family. He didn't become King Edward VII until 1901, at the age of sixty, so presumably he was able to party like a prince for quite some time. This recipe showed up in a tell-all memoir written by "a member of the royal household" titled *The Private Life of King Edward VII.* The drink is a bit of a mash-up—a cherry bounce mixed with a French 75. And if you use fine champagne, the drink will be fit for a king.

1 teaspoon simple syrup
1 dash Angostura bitters
1½ oz. rye whiskey
½ teaspoon maraschino liqueur
½ oz. lemon juice

1 chunk pineapple
1 oz. champagne
Glass: cocktail or coupe
Garnish: twist of lemon peel

Add simple syrup, bitters, rye, maraschino
liqueur, lemon juice, and pineapple chunk to a
cocktail shaker. Muddle the ingredients together,
add ice to the shaker, and shake vigorously for
60 seconds. Strain into a glass, top with champagne, and garnish with a lemon twist.

## Blood & Sand

This cocktail, which dates to circa 1922 London, is
named after the Rudolph Valentino film of the same
name. It's a tragic tale of a bullfighter who cheats on his
wife, reconciles with her, and then dies.

¾ oz. scotch
¾ oz. sweet vermouth
¾ oz. Cherry Heering liqueur
¾ oz. fresh orange juice
Glass: coupe or martini
Garnish: orange twist

Place all the ingredients in a shaker filled with
ice and shake for about 30 seconds. Double-
strain into a glass and express the orange twist
before dropping it into the drink.

## Cameron's Kick

This cocktail was created by Scottish bartender Harry
MacElhone at Ciro's Club in London. It first appeared in
his 1922 book *"Harry" of Ciro's ABC of Mixing Cocktails*

and then reappeared in his 1927 book *Barflies and Cocktails.* MacElhone took the cocktail with him to the New York Bar in Paris, where it became a favorite of Ernest Hemingway, Humphrey Bogart, and Rita Hayworth. His recipe was ⅓ scotch, ⅓ Irish whiskey, ⅙ lemon juice, and ⅙ orgeat syrup. Here's a modern interpretation:

1 oz. scotch
1 oz. Irish whiskey
½ oz. fresh lemon juice
½ oz. orgeat syrup
Glass: rocks
Garnish: lemon peel

Place all the ingredients in a shaker filled with ice and shake for 30 seconds. Double-strain into a rocks glass filled with ice and garnish with lemon peel.

## Whiskey Algonquin (or just the Algonquin)

Named after a New York hotel made famous by guests such as Dorothy Parker, Harpo Marx, and Alexander Woollcott, this drink is a mash-up of a Manhattan and a whiskey sour, but with pineapple juice instead of lemon juice. Interestingly, this cocktail dates back to Prohibition, and the Algonquin Hotel was dry at the time. Although the owner supported the temperance movement, the guests who frequented the hotel's dining room and became known as the Algonquin Round Table most decidedly did not. So of course, the drink that came to honor their discourse was not a mocktail.

1½ oz. rye
¾ oz. dry vermouth or blanc vermouth (a
    sweeter white vermouth)
¾ oz. fresh pineapple juice
1 or 2 dashes Peychaud's bitters or orange bitters
Glass: coupe or martini
Garnish: fresh pineapple or orange peel

Shake all the ingredients together for 30 to 60
seconds. Strain into a glass and add garnish.

## The Brown Derby

This cocktail was invented in the early 1930s at a trendy
Los Angeles hot spot called the Vendôme Club.

2 oz. bourbon
¾ oz. fresh grapefruit juice
¾ oz. honey syrup
Glass: rocks or coupe
Garnish: grapefruit wedge or wheel

Place all the ingredients in a shaker filled with
ice and shake for 60 seconds. Strain into a rocks
glass filled with ice or serve neat in a coupe.
Add garnish.

## Miami Beach Cocktail

Similar to the Brown Derby but invented across the
country in Florida, this Prohibition-era cocktail is a
combination of a sour cocktail and a Rob Roy or a
Manhattan made with scotch.

1 oz. scotch
1 oz. dry vermouth
1 oz. white grapefruit juice

Glass: cocktail or coupe
Garnish: grapefruit or lemon peel

Place all the ingredients in a shaker filled with
ice and shake for 60 seconds. Strain into a glass
and garnish with citrus peel.

### The Scofflaw

This is another riff of a Manhattan and a whiskey sour.
It was invented during Prohibition at Harry's New York
Bar in Paris.

2 oz. rye or bourbon
1 oz. dry vermouth
¼ oz. lemon juice
¼ teaspoon grenadine
1 or 2 dashes orange
   bitters
Glass: martini or coupe
Garnish: lemon or orange peel

Place all the ingredients in a shaker filled with
ice and shake vigorously for 60 seconds. Strain
into a glass and garnish with citrus peel.

### Scarlett O'Hara Cocktail

Long before Carrie and her friends started sipping
cosmopolitans at swanky bars in *Sex and the City*, fans
of *Gone with the Wind* swooned over Scarlett O'Hara
cocktails in the 1930s.

2 oz. Southern Comfort
1 oz. cranberry juice
1 oz. lime juice
Glass: martini or coupe

Garnish: lime wedge, wheel, or twist and 2 fresh
    or dried cranberries

Place all the ingredients in a shaker filled
with ice and shake vigorously for 60 seconds.
Strain into a glass and garnish with lime and
cranberries.

Note: To make this more of a whiskey cocktail
rather than a whiskey liqueur cocktail, replace
the Southern Comfort with Old Camp peach
pecan whiskey.

## Halekulani

Although most tiki drinks are made with rum, the
Halekulani is a classic tiki cocktail with a whiskey base.
It is believed that this tropical version of a whiskey
daiquiri was created at the Halekulani Hotel sometime
during the 1930s.

   1½ oz. bourbon, preferably overproof
   ½ oz. pineapple juice
   ½ oz. lemon juice
   ½ oz. orange juice
   ½ oz. demerara or rich sugar syrup
   ½ teaspoon grenadine
   1 dash Angostura or aromatic bitters
   Glass: old-fashioned or coupe
   Garnish: pineapple wedge and cherry

Combine all the ingredients in a shaker filled
with ice and shake for 30 to 60 seconds. Strain
into an old-fashioned glass filled with ice or a
coupe glass and add garnish.

## Wisconsin Whiskey Old-Fashioned Sour

Wisconsin bartenders have a unique way of making and serving old-fashioneds. If you order one in that state, the bartender will ask you some questions: brandy (Wisconsin's preferred spirit) or whiskey? Sweet or sour? Then she or he will proceed to muddle cherries, oranges, Angostura bitters, and spirit before topping it off with a sweet soda like Sprite or a sour soda like Squirt. A Wisconsin old-fashioned, especially one made with whiskey and a sour soda, is basically a modified whiskey sour. It dates back to the 1940s, although the muddled fruit was likely added earlier during Prohibition, when bad booze had to be made more palatable.

2 oz. whiskey, preferably bourbon
2 cherries
2 slices orange
3 dashes Angostura bitters
¼ to ¾ oz. simple syrup or 1 to 3 sugar cubes,
    depending on sweetness preference
3 to 5 oz. sour soda
Glass: rocks
Garnish: cherry and orange wedge

In the bottom of a cocktail shaker, muddle whiskey, cherries, orange slices, Angostura bitters, and simple syrup or sugar cubes. Top with ice. Either shake for 60 seconds or roll from one half of the shaker to the other until mixed. Pour directly into a glass without straining, top with soda, and add garnish.

Note: Instead of a sour soda like Squirt, I prefer to use a grapefruit soda such as TopNote or

Ω Mixers. Using a more refined soda makes this cocktail taste divine.

## Wisconsin Whiskey Slush

Slushes are Wisconsin's summertime drink, and although a few distilleries and bars serve them, this is typically a party drink served at backyard barbecues and tailgate gatherings. They are usually made with brandy (like the majority of Wisconsin old-fashioneds), but some people prefer whiskey. They date back to the 1960s or 1970s.

8 cups brewed black, green, or flavored tea
   (peach is a favorite)
1 cup sugar
12 oz. can orange juice concentrate
12 oz. can lemonade concentrate
2 cups whiskey
Lemon-lime soda
Glass: pint or plastic cups
Garnish: orange or lemon wedges or wheels
   (optional)

Brew 8 cups tea. Stir in sugar until dissolved and let cool. Stir together tea, orange juice concentrate, lemonade concentrate, and whiskey; pour into a container; and freeze for 24 to 48 hours. Because of the alcohol, it won't freeze solid but will turn into slush. To serve, place 1 or 2 scoops of slush in a cup, top with lemon-lime soda, and add garnish if desired. Makes 20 to 24 drinks.

## Whiskey Lemonade

This is basically a cheater's version of a whiskey sour—it's just lemonade and whiskey. In Kentucky, this is typically made with bourbon, and Jim Beam even came out with a line of canned cocktails called Kentucky Coolers, which are basically lemonade and bourbon with either fruity flavorings or tea. You can make a big batch in pitchers for summer parties or casual get-togethers. It's easy and delicious.

> 4 oz. lemonade
> 2 oz. bourbon
> Glass: pint or Collins
> Garnish: lemon wedge or wheel

> Shake bourbon and lemonade together in a shaker filled with ice for about 30 seconds or until chilled. Strain into a glass filled with ice and add lemon garnish.

## Lynchburg Lemonade

This version of whiskey lemonade is made with Tennessee whiskey, and given that Jack Daniel's is located in Lynchburg, it's not surprising that the company features this recipe—which led to a lawsuit.

Despite its name, Lynchburg lemonade was created in 1980 by a bartender named Tony Mason in Huntsville, Alabama. In 1982 Jack Daniel's developed a promotional campaign that used Mason's proprietary recipe, and in 1987 he sued. Even though Mason won the case, he wasn't awarded any punitive damages, and to this day, Jack Daniel's still features the recipe on its website. And no wonder—it's a delicious riff on the whiskey sour. The original recipe used a 1980s sour mix, but fresh lemon juice and simple syrup make a better version.

> 1 oz. Jack Daniel's or other Tennessee whiskey
> 1 oz. triple sec or other orange liqueur
> ½ oz. fresh lemon juice
> ½ oz. simple syrup
> 4 oz. lemon-lime soda
> Glass: mason jar, Collins, or pint
> Garnish: lemon wedge

> Pour whiskey, orange liqueur, lemon juice, and simple syrup into a cocktail shaker filled with ice. Shake for 30 seconds or until well chilled. Strain into a glass and garnish with lemon.

## Gold Rush

This modern classic was invented by T. J. Siegel at the Milk & Honey bar in New York City when a patron requested that his whiskey sour be made with the honey syrup the bar used in daiquiris.

> 2 oz. bourbon
> ¾ oz. fresh lemon juice
> ¾ oz. honey syrup (see the recipe in chapter 4)
> Glass: rocks
> Garnish: lemon peel

> Place all the ingredients in a shaker filled with ice and shake for 60 seconds. Strain into a rocks glass filled with ice or with 1 large ice cube. Garnish with lemon peel.

## Penicillin

This cocktail was created at Milk & Honey by mixologist Sam Ross. Like the Gold Rush, the Penicillin has become a modern classic—some call it the best classic of the century.

2 oz. blended scotch
¾ oz. lemon juice
¾ oz. honey-ginger syrup (see the recipe in chapter 4)
¼ oz. single-malt Islay scotch
Glass: rocks
Garnish: candied ginger

Place the blended scotch, lemon juice, and honey-ginger syrup in a shaker filled with ice and shake for 60 seconds. Strain into a rocks glass filled with ice, top with single-malt Islay scotch poured over the back of a bar spoon, and garnish with candied ginger.

Note: Some recipes add ¼ oz. ginger liqueur, in which case you should replace the honey-ginger syrup with honey syrup and reduce the amount to ½ oz.

## Paper Plane

This cocktail was invented by Sam Ross for the Violet Hour in Chicago. It's a modern twist on the Last Word, which is equal parts gin, maraschino liqueur, green Chartreuse, and lime juice. It's also a balanced yet bitter twist on the whiskey sour.

¾ oz. bourbon
¾ oz. Aperol
¾ oz. Amaro Nonino Quintessentia
¾ oz. fresh lemon juice
Glass: coupe or martini
Garnish: lemon twist and small paper airplane

Place all the ingredients in a shaker filled with ice and shake for 30 to 60 seconds. Strain into a glass and add garnish.

Note: Aperol is a bitter aperitif that is similar to Campari. Amaro Nonino Quintessentia is an Italian bitter liqueur (*amaro* means "little bitter") that's made by infusing grappa with botanicals and herbs. If you can't find it, you can substitute a different Italian amaro, Cynar, Chartreuse, or Angostura liqueur, but it won't taste the same.

## Smash Cocktails

Smash cocktails might seem like a modern riff—especially when they're made with herbs—but they actually date back to the nineteenth century. Smashes are related to fix cocktails, and fixes were basically sours dressed with the fruit of the season, whereas smashes muddled the fruit.

Historically, smashes were made with quince, blackberries, cherries, and peaches, but almost any fruit that is easily mashed can be muddled into a smash, including strawberries, melons, and raspberries. Harder fruits like apples and pears don't work well.

### Blackberry-Sage Smash
4 fresh sage leaves
4 fresh blackberries

2 oz. rye or other whiskey
¾ oz. lemon juice
¾ oz. simple syrup
2 or 3 dashes Angostura bitters
Glass: coupe
Garnish: fresh blackberries

Muddle all the ingredients in the bottom of a cocktail shaker. Add ice and shake for 30 to 60 seconds. Strain into a glass and garnish with blackberries.

Note: You can easily switch up the fruit and the herbs or omit the herbs entirely. Try strawberries and basil, peaches and mint, raspberries and rosemary, blueberries and thyme—the combinations are endless.

## Rye-Tai

This is a whiskey version of the classic tiki drink the mai tai. If you love whiskey and the tropics, this is the cocktail for you.

2 oz. rye or other whiskey
1 oz. lime juice
½ oz. orange liqueur
½ oz. orgeat
2 or 3 dashes orange bitters
Glass: tiki or poco grande
Garnish: 2 mint sprigs

Fill a shaker with ice. Add all the ingredients and shake for 30 to 60 seconds. Strain into a glass filled with ice. Take 1 sprig of mint and gently rub it around the rim of the glass; then discard. Take the remaining mint sprig, spank it (hit it quickly between your hands to lightly crush and bring out the aromatics), and use it to garnish the drink.

Note: You can reduce the lime juice to ½ oz. and add ½ oz. lemon juice or pineapple juice if desired.

## AK-47 Cocktail

If you like a drink that knocks you out, or at least knocks you over, the AK-47 might be for you. It's similar to a Long Island iced tea, in that it combines a medley of booze that's topped with bubbles—rum, vodka, gin, tequila, and triple sec, plus lemon juice, simple syrup, and cola. The AK-47 is even more potent—gin, vodka, rum, scotch, bourbon, brandy, and Cointreau or orange liqueur, plus lime juice and soda water. In any case, many modern renditions include the warning to "drink responsibly."

⅓ oz. scotch
⅓ oz. bourbon
⅓ oz. brandy
⅓ oz. rum
⅓ oz. gin
⅓ oz. vodka
⅓ oz. Cointreau or other orange liqueur
⅓ oz. fresh lime juice
4 to 6 oz. club soda or seltzer water
Glass: pint or Collins
Garnish: lime wheel or wedge

Combine the scotch, bourbon, brandy, rum, gin, vodka, Cointreau or orange liqueur, and lime juice in the bottom of a shaker and stir until chilled. Pour into a glass filled with ice, top with club soda or seltzer water, and stir until combined. Garnish with lime.

## Whiskeyrita

The margarita typically ranks among the top five cocktails in the United States, but since most American distilleries do not make tequilas or agave-based spirits, a whiskey version of the margarita was created: the Whiskeyrita. The cocktail has shown up on blogs and in Mexican restaurants.

2 oz. whiskey
¾ oz. orange liqueur
¾ oz. fresh lime juice
¼ oz. agave nectar
Glass: rocks, margarita, or martini
Garnish: lime wedge or wheel and salt

Run a lime wedge around the rim of a glass; then dip it in salt. Place all the ingredients in a shaker filled with ice and shake vigorously for 30 seconds. Double-strain into the prepared glass filled with ice and add garnish.

# 6

# Juicy Riffs

One of the easiest riffs on a whiskey sour is to replace the traditional lemon juice with another juice or juices. However, most other juice-based whiskey sours still need a splash of lemon juice. The exception is a lime whiskey sour. Because lime juice and lemon juice have very similar sugar and citric acid levels, they can be used interchangeably. Even better, mix equal parts lemon and lime juice. The commingling of the two juices makes a lovely whiskey sour with a bit more depth. Another simple riff is to use Meyer lemon juice, which gives the cocktail an almost floral aroma and is quite delicious.

Grapefruit, orange, and pineapple juice all have more sugar than lemon juice, so if you use any of these juices—as well as cranberry, apple, and other juices—use ¼ to ½ ounce of your juice of choice, along with ¼ to ½ ounce lemon juice, depending on your taste. As a general rule, the less sour the other fruit, the more lemon juice needed to balance the whiskey sour. If you're not sure about the proportions, add lemon juice in increments of ¼ ounce. In addition, you might want to decrease the amount of sugar or simple syrup in the cocktail when using fruits with higher sugar contents.

You can also combine more than one other juice with lemon juice in a whiskey sour. Orange and pineapple work well together, for example—use ¼ ounce of each. Another great combination is lime and cranberry.

Try any or all of the following juicy riffs to vary your whiskey sour cocktails.

## Citrusy Riffs

Note that when switching the citrus in a whiskey sour, you can also vary the bitters. Instead of Angostura or aromatic bitters, use orange bitters or a combination of orange and Angostura bitters. Fee Brothers and Scrappy's also make grapefruit bitters, lemon bitters, and lime bitters, and Yes Cocktail Company makes Meyer lemon bitters. If you like, you can even make your own citrus bitters.

Most of the following recipes use the golden formula (see chapter 2), but feel free to use your own favorite formula. For each of these cocktails, you could add 2 drops of saline solution (see chapter 3), bitters, and egg white or egg white substitute. If you use both bitters and egg white, the instructions change: shake all the ingredients except bitters in a cocktail shaker without ice for 30 seconds. Then add ice and shake for another 30 to 60 seconds. Double-strain into a glass and top with bitters before adding garnish.

### Meyer Lemon Whiskey Sour

This is the easiest citrus riff, and it has a lovely floral aroma.

2 oz. whiskey
¾ oz. Meyer lemon juice
¾ oz. simple syrup
Glass: rocks
Garnish: cherry and Meyer lemon wheel

Place all the ingredients in a shaker with ice and shake for 60 seconds. Double-strain into a glass and add garnish.

**Lime Whiskey Sour**

This sour tastes a little bit like Florida.

2 oz. whiskey
¾ oz. lime juice
¾ oz. simple syrup
Glass: rocks
Garnish: cherry and lime wedge

Place all the ingredients in a shaker with ice and shake for 60 seconds. Double-strain into a glass and add garnish.

**Lemon-Lime Whiskey Sour**

This is one of the best sour combinations. It has a bit more depth than a traditional whiskey sour and is a definite crowd pleaser.

2 oz. whiskey
¾ oz. simple syrup
¾ oz. fresh lime-lemon juice blend (instructions follow)
Glass: rocks
Garnish: cherry, lemon wedge, lime wedge

Place all the ingredients in a shaker with ice and shake for 30 to 60 seconds. Double-strain into a glass and add garnish.

To make the lemon-lime juice blend, whisk together 2 oz. of each. Then measure out the amount you need and refrigerate the rest for up to 3 days or freeze for up to a month.

### Orange Whiskey Sour

2 oz. whiskey
¾ oz. simple syrup
½ oz. fresh orange juice
¼ fresh lemon juice
Glass: rocks
Garnish: cherry and orange wedge

Place all the ingredients in a shaker with ice and shake for 30 to 60 seconds. Double-strain into a glass and add garnish.

Note: Other options include a blood orange or Cara Cara orange whiskey sour.

### Grapefruit Whiskey Sour

This is a lovely cocktail to serve at brunch. It's a good accompaniment to grapefruit halves coated with a mixture of butter, bitters, and brown sugar and then broiled for a minute or two.

2 oz. whiskey
¾ oz. simple syrup
½ oz. fresh grapefruit juice
¼ oz. fresh lemon juice
3 dashes Angostura or citrus bitters
Glass: rocks
Garnish: cherry and grapefruit wedge

Place all the ingredients in a shaker with ice and shake for 30 to 60 seconds Double-strain into a glass and add garnish.

Note: Grapefruit juice can be pretty sour (although the pink variety is less so). If you like your whiskey sours on the sweet side, use ¾ oz. grapefruit juice and omit the lemon juice.

**Stitzel Sour**
*Courtesy of Blade and Bow Kentucky Straight Bourbon Whiskey*
This recipe combines three different citrus juices into one refreshing whiskey sour cocktail.

1¼ oz. Blade and Bow Kentucky straight bourbon whiskey
½ oz. fresh lemon juice
¼ oz. fresh grapefruit juice
¼ oz. fresh lime juice
½ oz. simple syrup
Glass: rocks
Garnish: maraschino cherry and orange peel

Pour bourbon, fresh juices, and simple syrup into a shaker filled with ice and shake for 30 seconds. Strain into a rocks glass filled with ice and add garnish.

## Other Fruity Riffs

**Pineapple Whiskey Sour**
This whiskey sour is suitable for tiki parties everywhere.

2 oz. whiskey
¾ oz. simple syrup
½ oz. fresh pineapple juice
¼ oz. fresh lemon juice
Glass: rocks
Garnish: cherry and pineapple wedge

Place all the ingredients in a shaker with ice and shake for 30 to 60 seconds. Double-strain into a glass and add garnish.

Note: If the pineapple is very fresh and sweet, you might want to reduce the simple syrup to ½ oz.

Variations: Substitute lime juice for the lemon juice for an even tikier vibe. For a pineapple-orange whiskey sour, use ¼ oz. each pineapple, orange, and lemon juice.

### Cranberry Whiskey Sour

This is a great sour to serve around the holidays.

2 oz. whiskey
½ oz. 100 percent cranberry juice
¼ oz. lemon juice
¾ oz. simple syrup
Glass: rocks
Garnish: cherry wrapped in a lemon peel or a
    few fresh cranberries

Place all the ingredients in a shaker with ice and shake for 60 seconds. Double-strain into a glass and add garnish.

Note: For a more intense cranberry flavor, combine 1 cup whiskey and 1 cup fresh cranberries in a mason jar. Let the cranberries steep for a month until the whiskey is a bright red color. Then use this whiskey to make your whiskey sour.

**Apple Whiskey Sour**

This whiskey sour is perfect for autumn, and it's ripe for riffing. Cinnamon simple syrup, honey-ginger simple syrup, or any spiced simple syrup works well. A ¼-ounce float of chai liqueur or apple liqueur is also quite nice.

2 oz. whiskey
½ oz. simple syrup
½ oz. fresh apple cider
¼ to ½ oz. fresh lemon juice
Glass: rocks
Garnish: apple wedge

Place all the ingredients in a shaker with ice and shake for 30 to 60 seconds. Double-strain into a glass and add garnish.

Note: I would go with the higher amount of lemon juice (½ oz.), but other tasters preferred less. You be the judge.

**Pomegranate Whiskey Sour**

2 oz. whiskey
½ oz. pomegranate juice
¼ oz. lemon juice
½ to ¾ oz. simple syrup
Glass: rocks
Garnish: cherry wrapped in a lemon peel or a
    few fresh cranberries

Place all the ingredients in a shaker with ice and shake for 60 seconds. Double-strain into a glass and add garnish.

Note: In my opinion, the pomegranate juice is sweet enough to use just ½ oz. simple syrup. If you want even more pomegranate flavor, use a homemade grenadine syrup.

**Lychee Sour**
Fresh lychees are sometimes available at specialty grocery stores, but canned lychees are available year-round. This sweet-sour fruit has a delicious aroma and adds a subtle note to a whiskey sour. It works very well with Japanese whiskies.

2 oz. whiskey
½ oz. lychee liquid from canned lychee fruit or fresh lychee juice
½ oz. lemon juice
½ oz. simple syrup
Glass: coupe or martini
Garnish: lychee fruit

Place all the ingredients in a shaker with ice and shake for 30 to 60 seconds. Double-strain into a coupe or martini glass and add garnish.

Note: This cocktail tastes sublime when egg whites and orange or citrus bitters are added.

**Blackberry Smash**

*Amy Wimmer, Del-Bar, Wisconsin Dells, Wisconsin*

This modern smash combines mint and blackberries for a refreshing fruity sour.

2 oz. Basil Hayden bourbon

¾ oz. lime juice

¾ oz. simple syrup

3 or 4 fresh blackberries

3 or 4 mint leaves

Glass: rocks

Garnish: fresh blackberries on a skewer and sprig of fresh mint

Place all the ingredients except the mint leaves in the bottom of a cocktail shaker and muddle the blackberries. Add the mint and, using the muddler, gently press to express the oils. Add ice and shake for 30 seconds. Double-strain into a rocks glass filled with ice. Gently spank the mint sprig between your hands to release its aromatics before placing it in the glass and adding the skewer of blackberries.

# 7

# Modern Riffs

**M**odern mixologists have come up with all sorts of interesting variations on the whiskey sour—adding liqueurs, creating different syrups, and infusing whiskeys with unique flavors. Some of these recipes are pretty easy to make at home, while others require patience and specialized ingredients. But they're all delicious.

**Standard Sour**
*Pat McQuillan, cofounder, Central Standard Distillery, Milwaukee, Wisconsin*
"At Central Standard, our inspiration is the spirit of the outdoors and the relaxing Midwest style," says McQuillan, explaining why Central Standard Distillery has created spirits such as Red Cabin bourbon, WI North brandy, and Door County cherry vodka. "We wanted to bring the celebration of the outdoors to life in this twist on the classic whiskey sour." In McQuillan's recipe, the rosemary elevates the cocktail's herbal notes, and the blackberries offset the "sharp-sour" taste of the lemon juice while adding a bright burgundy color. "We envision the Standard Sour being enjoyed by the campfire, on the lake, or as a dinner cocktail with friends and family," he says.

1½ oz. Red Cabin bourbon

½ oz. rosemary simple syrup (see the recipe in chapter 4)

1 oz. lemon juice

2 blackberries

1 egg white

Glass: rocks

Garnish: blackberry and rosemary sprig

Pour the rosemary syrup into the bottom of a cocktail shaker, add the blackberries, and muddle the berries. Add lemon juice, bourbon, egg white, and ice and shake for 30 seconds. Strain out the ice, then dry-shake for another 30 seconds. Double-strain into a rocks glass filled with ice and add garnish.

### Rose Royale

*Jane Danger, mixologist, Pernod Ricard*

This whiskey sour is basically a whiskey version of the French 75. It's a romantic cocktail, perfect for Valentine's Day. "It's always fun to do something unexpected that you would not normally think of when you're thinking of whiskey cocktails," Danger says. "The inspiration for this cocktail comes from my longtime love of sparkling wine and champagne. I also wanted a cocktail that would work seasonally for the holidays and for spring."

1½ oz. Glenlivet 12-year-old scotch infused with rose tea (instructions follow)

¾ oz. honey syrup

¾ oz. lemon juice

2 oz. Mumm Napa Sparkling Brut rosé wine
Glass: short goblet or stemmed rocks glass
Garnish: edible rose petals

Pour scotch, honey syrup, and lemon juice into a shaker filled with ice. Shake for 30 seconds. Strain into a glass, top with wine, and garnish with rose petals.

To infuse the scotch, pour 1 cup (8 oz.) scotch into a nonreactive container with 1½ tablespoons rose tea. Let it sit for 2 to 4 hours; then fine-strain.

### Plop Jai in Phuket
*Kira Webster, beverage director, Indo and Nippon Tei, St. Louis, Missouri*
In Thai, *plop jai* means "solace," and Phuket is the largest island in Thailand. Webster began serving this cocktail in the late fall and expected to keep it on the menu through early winter, but it was so popular that she served it until late spring. "It is such a bright cocktail," she says. "I was really proud I came up with it."

1 oz. Barbadillo Fino sherry
1 oz. aquafaba
¾ oz. persimmon-infused Knob Creek rye
    (instructions follow)
½ oz. lemon juice
½ oz. Big O ginger liqueur
¼ oz. vanilla syrup (see the recipe in chapter 4)
1 dash chocolate bitters
Glass: coupe
Garnish: coconut spice mix (recipe follows)

Place all the ingredients in a shaker without ice and dry-shake for 30 seconds. Add ice and shake for another 30 seconds. Double-strain into a glass and add garnish.

To infuse the rye, blend it with persimmons in a food processor until well mixed. Let it sit for 10 minutes; then fine-strain the persimmons out. If you want more persimmon flavor, let it infuse overnight.

### Coconut Spice Mix
3 tablespoons coconut flakes
½ teaspoon sugar
½ teaspoon salt
⅛ teaspoon cinnamon
⅛ teaspoon black pepper

Grind all ingredients in a Vitamix or high-speed blender.

### Sour Saru
*Kira Webster, beverage director, Indo and Nippon Tei, St. Louis, Missouri*
Webster is one of the most creative bartenders around, and this sour has a lot of depth. *Saru* means "monkey" in Japanese.

1¼ oz. Monkey Shoulder scotch
1 oz. oleo saccharum
½ oz. Amaro Averna
½ oz. China-China Amer liqueur
½ oz. simple syrup
½ oz. fresh lemon juice
½ oz. fresh lime juice
½ oz. aquafaba

4 dashes Japanese umami bitters
Glass: big coupe
Garnish: Thai basil leaf

Place all the ingredients in a shaker and shake for 30 seconds. Add ice and shake for another 30 seconds. Double-strain into a glass and add garnish on top.

Note: Amaro Averna is a popular Italian bitter liqueur (*amaro* means "little bitter" in Italian). Made of a complex blend of herbs, flowers, and spices, it has a bittersweet taste with notes of orange, licorice, juniper, and rosemary. China-China Amer liqueur is made with sweet and bitter orange peels. It has a bitter orange peel and licorice taste, with cinnamon and cardamom aromas.

### Mistletoe
*Amanda Beckwith, lead blender and education manager, Virginia Distillery Co., Lovingston, Virginia*

Beckwith created this cocktail for a holiday party at the distillery, and everyone clamored for the recipe. "It's so pretty with that bright red color," she says. "It's got just a little bit of herbaceousness to it."

1½ oz. Virginia Highland malt whisky
1½ oz. cinnamon, sage, and cranberry syrup
   (see the recipe in chapter 4)

½ oz. lemon juice
½ oz. lime juice
½ oz. orange juice
2 dashes orange bitters
Glass: rocks
Garnish: 2 or 3 sugarcoated cranberries (see the
    recipe in chapter 4)

Place whiskey, syrup, and juices in a shaker
filled with ice and shake vigorously for 30 to
60 seconds, or until the shaker is completely
frosted. Double-strain into a rocks glass filled
with ice, top with orange bitters, and garnish
with cranberries.

**The Neighborhood Bully**
*Andy Knuth, general manager, Cobblestone Restau-
rant and Cider Bar, Chicago, Illinois*
This cocktail was inspired by local writer Bull
Darlington, a whiskey aficionado. The cocktail
originated from a conversation among Darlington, Knuth, and Caleb, the bar manager. "Whiskey has always been a passion of mine," says
Knuth, "and the presentation of whiskey cocktails
was never quite the eye-catching experience I
had hoped for." But adding mint "transforms a
dull-colored liquor into a quick thing of beauty."
Knuth admits, "Bull Darlington is the creator of
the name. I cannot take credit for that."

1½ oz. whiskey
¾ oz. fresh lemon juice
½ oz. simple syrup
Glass: rocks
Garnish: fresh mint

Place all the ingredients in a shaker filled with ice and shake vigorously until chilled, about 30 seconds. Double-strain into a rocks glass filled with ice. Gently hit the mint in your hands to release its oils and add it to the drink.

**Boggy Sour**
*Brendan Cleary, bar manager, Great Lakes Distillery, Milwaukee, Wisconsin*
This is a fresh and fruity whiskey sour.

2 oz. Still & Oak rye
½ oz. Good Land cranberry liqueur
½ oz. simple syrup or demerara syrup
1 oz. fresh lemon juice
2 dashes grapefruit bitters
Glass: rocks
Garnish: lemon wheel

Place all the ingredients in a shaker filled with ice and shake for at least 30 seconds. Double-strain into a rocks glass filled with ice and add garnish.

**Door County Sour**
*Brendan Cleary, bar manager, Great Lakes Distillery, Milwaukee, Wisconsin*
This grapefruit sour is reminiscent of a Paloma.

1 oz. Still & Oak bourbon
1 oz. Good Land cherry liqueur
5 oz. Top Note grapefruit soda
Glass: highball
Garnish: lemon wedge

Stir all the ingredients together in a highball glass and garnish with a lemon wedge.

## Rye Whiskey Slush

*Brendan Cleary, bar manager, Great Lakes Distillery, Milwaukee, Wisconsin*

Slushes are some of the most popular cocktails Cleary makes. "I yell 'service' and pour this cocktail to everyone who comes running," he says.

6 oz. Still & Oak bourbon
12 oz. can orange juice concentrate
3 oz. fresh lemon juice
2 oz. fresh lime juice
2 oz. Good Land cherry liqueur
2 oz. agave syrup
10 dashes Angostura bitters
3 cups ice
Glass: highball
Garnish: citrus wheel

Pour all the ingredients into a heavy-duty blender and blend until smooth. Makes 3 to 4 cocktails.

## Old Market Sour

*Upstream Brewing Company, Omaha, Nebraska*

This is a fun and flavorful version of a New York sour.

1½ oz. Evan Williams 1786 whiskey or other whiskey
½ oz. Licor 43 or other orange liqueur
½ oz. fresh lemon juice

½ oz. cinnamon simple syrup (see the recipe in
   chapter 4)
1 oz. Camelot cabernet sauvignon
Glass: rocks
Garnish: orange peel (optional)

Place whiskey, Licor 43, lemon juice, and cinnamon simple syrup in a shaker filled with ice and
shake for 30 to 60 seconds. Strain into a rocks
glass filled with ice. Pour wine on top over the
back of a bar spoon. Add garnish if desired.

**Amendment 30**
*30 Hop, Cedar Rapids, Iowa*
This cocktail is a cross between a whiskey sour
and a whiskey mule, and it's delicious.

1½ oz. Four Roses bourbon or
   other bourbon
½ oz. Canton ginger liqueur or
   other ginger liqueur
2 oz. sour mix (equal parts lemon
   juice and simple syrup)
3 dashes peach bitters
¼ to ½ oz. ginger beer
Glass: rocks
Garnish: Luxardo cherry

Place all the ingredients except the ginger beer
in a shaker filled with ice and shake for 30 to
60 seconds. Strain into a rocks glass filled with
ice. Top with a splash of ginger beer and add
garnish.

## Sly Rabbit

*Jason Van Auken, general manager and beverage director, Brandywine Restaurant, Cedarburg, Wisconsin*

You might not think carrot juice belongs in a whiskey sour, but Van Auken proves that it does. This cocktail will knock your socks off.

1¼ oz. Bulleit bourbon
1 oz. Cardamaro
⅓ oz. Aperol
1½ oz. fresh carrot juice
⅓ oz. demerara syrup
½ oz. fresh lemon juice
1 oz. Langunitas Hoppy Refresher
Glass: rocks
Garnish: thyme sprigs

Place all the ingredients except the Hoppy Refresher in a shaker filled with ice and shake vigorously for 30 seconds. Put an infused ice cube (instructions follow) into a rocks glass, double-strain the cocktail into the glass, pour Hoppy Refresher on top, and add garnish.

To make infused ice, prepare butterfly pea tea according to the directions (about 1 teaspoon tea per 1 cup water). Cool a bit and then stir in at least 2 oz. lemon juice to change the color of the tea (from blue to purple). Pour into a large ice cube tray with a sprig or two of thyme in each cube.

## Old World Sour

*Fitz Bailey, brand ambassador, Brown-Forman*
*Distillery, Louisville, Kentucky*

"I really wanted to find a way to add a little more flavor to this cocktail without overwhelming anything," Bailey says. Using the leftover syrup from Luxardo cherries, he created a cocktail with an extra tart cherry note and a velvety purple color. "It's such an eye-catching and easy-to-drink beverage," he says, "even with the 100-proof bourbon in it. It just evaporates in your glass."

1½ oz. Coopers' Craft Barrel Reserve 100-proof
    bourbon
½ oz. fresh lemon juice
½ oz. fresh lime juice
¾ oz. Luxardo cherry syrup
1 egg white
Glass: rocks
Garnish: Luxardo cherry

Pour egg white into a shaker and dry-shake for 10 to 20 seconds. Pour in the other ingredients and shake for 20 to 30 seconds. Add ice and shake for another 20 to 30 seconds. Double-strain into a rocks glass filled with ice and add a cherry.

## Fall Whiskey Sour

*Fitz Bailey, brand ambassador, Brown-Forman*
*Distillery, Louisville, Kentucky*

This is one of Bailey's most popular sour recipes, especially in autumn, and it's delicious.

1½ oz. Coopers' Barrel Reserve bourbon (100 proof)
1 oz. fresh lemon juice
½ oz. maple syrup
1 egg white
Glass: rocks
Garnish: maple leaf or candy corn

Pour egg white into a shaker and dry-shake for 10 to 20 seconds. Pour in the other ingredients and shake for 20 to 30 seconds. Add ice and shake for another 20 to 30 seconds. Double-strain into a rocks glass filled with ice and add garnish.

**Whiskey Amaretto Sour**
This is a good ease-into whiskey sour.

1½ oz. whiskey
½ oz. Amaretto or other almond liqueur
¾ oz. lemon juice
½ oz. orgeat
1 egg white
3 drops Angostura bitters
Glass: coupe
Garnish: dried orange wheel

Place all the ingredients except the bitters in a shaker and dry-shake for 30 to 60 seconds. Add ice and shake until chilled, 30 to 60 seconds. Double-strain into a glass, top with bitters, and add garnish.

Note: To make a variation, replace ¼ oz. lemon juice with fresh orange juice or, for a more colorful drink, use fresh blood orange juice.

**Christian Grey**

*Rhondi Love, owner of Edith Cocktail Bar, Milwaukee, Wisconsin*

The name of this Manhattan–whiskey sour mashup comes from the soundtrack of the *Fifty Shades of Grey* franchise, which sometimes plays at the bar. "It's a really good soundtrack," says Love.

1½ oz. bourbon
¼ oz. sweet vermouth
¼ oz. Italicus (bergamot rosolio or any type of Italian aperitivo)
¾ oz. lemon juice
¾ oz. Earl Grey tea syrup (substitute Earl Grey tea for Sweet Tea Simple Syrup recipe in chapter 4)
1 egg white
Glass: coupe
Garnish: finely crushed tea leaves and dehydrated lemon

Combine all the ingredients in a shaker. Dry-shake without ice. Add ice and shake again. Strain into glass, sprinkle tea leaves on top, and add dehydrated lemon.

**New World Sour**

*Starward Australian Whisky, Melbourne, Australia*

This Australian twist on a New York sour uses fresh cracked black pepper to bring out the spirit's tannic spice, which comes from storing it in Australian red wine barrels.

50 mL (1½ oz.) Starward Two-Fold Whisky
20 mL (4 teaspoons) fresh lemon juice
20 mL (4 teaspoons) simple syrup
1 egg white
15 mL (½ oz.) Australian shiraz wine
Fresh cracked black pepper
Glass: rocks
Garnish: none

Place all the ingredients except the shiraz in a cocktail shaker and add 1 turn of black pepper from a grinder. Shake without ice to emulsify the egg white, about 30 seconds. Add ice and shake vigorously for another 30 seconds. Strain into a rocks glass filled with fresh ice and float shiraz over the top.

Note: Alternatively, the measurements can be stated as 5 parts whiskey, 2 parts lemon juice, 2 parts simple syrup, and just under 2 parts wine.

**Breslauer Sour**
*Heimat Fruit Liqueurs, Mamaroneck, New York*
If you like fruity liqueurs, this is your kind of whiskey sour.

2½ oz. whiskey
1 oz. Heimat New York white peach liqueur or
    other peach liqueur
½ oz. lemon juice
¾ oz. Heimat raspberry or other raspberry liqueur
Glass: rocks
Garnish: peach or fresh raspberries

Pour all the ingredients except the raspberry liqueur into a shaker filled with ice and shake until cold, 30 to 60 seconds. Double-strain into a rocks glass filled with ice, pour raspberry liqueur down one side of the glass, and add garnish.

**Whiskey Stone Sour**
*Joe O'Brien, bartender, The Informalist, Hotel Lismore, Eau Claire, Wisconsin*
After having a lovely gin and aquavit sour, I asked the bartender to make me a riff on a whiskey sour. Joe O'Brien came up with this delicious recipe on the spot.

50 mL (1½ oz.) bourbon or whiskey
25 mL (5 teaspoons) fresh lemon juice
20 mL (4 teaspoons) fresh orange juice
20 mL (4 teaspoons) dry curaçao
1 teaspoon Grand Marnier
Glass: Collins
Garnish: orange zest

Shake all the ingredients except the Grand Marnier with ice for 30 to 60 seconds. Strain into a Collins glass filled with ice, garnish with a strip of orange zest, and pour a float of Grand Marnier on top.

**Rocky Mountain Marmalade**
*Stranahan Whiskey, Denver, Colorado*
This straightforward whiskey sour recipe is enhanced by just a touch of orange marmalade, giving it a sweet tang.

2 oz. Stranahan's Blue Peak Colorado whiskey
¾ oz. fresh lemon juice
¾ oz. simple syrup

Bar spoon of orange marmalade
Glass: rocks
Garnish: dehydrated orange wheel

Combine all the ingredients in a shaker filled with ice and shake for 30 seconds. Double-strain into a rocks glass over cubed ice and add garnish.

### Aldean Sour

*Wolf Moon Bourbon, Lawrenceburg, Indiana*
Created by country music stars Jason Aldean and Florida Georgia Line, this cocktail is for anyone who enjoys sweet tea in a sour.

2 oz. Wolf Moon bourbon
¾ oz. fresh lemon juice
¾ oz. sweet tea simple syrup (see the recipe in chapter 4)
Glass: rocks
Garnish: mint sprig

Combine all the ingredients in a shaker filled with ice. Shake vigorously for about 30 seconds. Double-strain into a rocks glass filled with ice and add garnish.

### Southern Sour

*Old Camp Peach Pecan Whiskey, Proximo Spirits, Jersey City, New Jersey*
If you like peaches, this is the whiskey sour for you.

2 oz. Old Camp Peach Pecan Whiskey
¾ oz. fresh lemon juice
¾ oz. simple syrup

2 peach slices
2 dashes Angostura bitters
Glass: rocks
Garnish: peach slice and mint sprig

Place the lemon juice, simple syrup, and peaches in the bottom of a cocktail shaker and muddle until the peaches are broken down. Add whiskey and ice and shake until chilled and diluted, 30 to 60 seconds. Pour straight into a glass without straining, top with bitters, and add garnish.

## Word of Advice

*Jason Lively, Tine Restaurant, Brattleboro, Vermont*
Lively calls this an egg white sour, but it plays with the idea of a boulevardier. "A word of advice usually comes from a place of kindness and compassion but it can often be bittersweet, and in the end you are usually happy to have received it," he says. The spirits provide a sweet richness and a touch of acidity and bitterness. The egg white softens the texture, and the bitters and cardamom sugar add spice and opulence. Together, it all adds up to "a balance of flavor sensations, texture, and aroma," says Lively.

2 oz. Saxtons Sapling Maple rye
1 oz. Orleans bitter aperitif cider
¼ oz. fresh lemon juice
½ oz. simple syrup
1 egg white
Peychaud's bitters
Glass: coupe
Garnish: cardamom sugar rim

To prepare the glass, mix 1 teaspoon powdered cardamom and 1 teaspoon raw sugar on a small plate or in a shallow dish. Wet the rim of a coupe glass with a piece of citrus and coat the rim with the dry mixture. Place all the ingredients except the bitters in a shaker and shake for about 30 seconds. Add ice and shake for another 30 seconds. Double-strain into the prepared glass. To finish, gently place 4 dots of Peychaud's bitters on the froth and, using a toothpick, draw a line through the dots to create a pretty swirl.

### Garden Sour

The combination of sugar snap peas and whiskey may sound a bit odd, but it's actually quite refreshing and has a lovely green hue.

2 oz. whiskey
½ oz. Midori or other melon liqueur
¾ oz. fresh lime juice
¾ oz. sugar snap pea and cilantro syrup (see the recipe in chapter 4)
½ oz. fresh egg white or aquafaba
1 dash orange bitters
1 dash aromatic or Angostura bitters
Glass: coupe or wide champagne glass
Garnish: lime wheel or sugar snap pea

Place all the ingredients in a shaker without ice and dry-shake for 60 seconds. Add ice and shake for another 60

seconds. Double-strain into a glass and add garnish,

**Five Keys Sour**
*Blade and Bow Kentucky Whiskey, Shively, Kentucky*
This recipe is a mash-up of an Arnold Palmer and a New York sour.

1¼ oz. Blade and Bow Kentucky straight bourbon whiskey
¾ oz. lemon juice
1 oz. simple syrup
1 dash orange bitters
½ oz. brewed hibiscus tea
Glass: double old-fashioned
Garnish: lemon wheel

Pour all the ingredients except the tea into a shaker filled with ice and shake for 30 seconds. Double-strain into a double old-fashioned glass filled with ice. Gently pour the tea onto the back of a bar spoon into the glass to float on top. Garnish with a lemon wheel.

**Kentucky Sour**
*Blade and Bow Kentucky Whiskey, Shively, Kentucky*
This elegant riff on a whiskey sour uses limoncello as a modifier.

1¼ oz. Blade and Bow Kentucky straight bourbon whiskey
¾ oz. limoncello liqueur
½ oz. orange juice
¼ oz. lemon juice
¼ oz. simple syrup

1 dash cranberry bitters
1 egg white
Glass: coupe or martini
Garnish: dehydrated blood orange or lemon peel

Place all the ingredients in a shaker and dry-shake for 30 seconds. Add ice and shake for another 30 seconds. Double-strain into a glass and add garnish.

### Ginger Sour
*Bill Foster, cofounder, Big O, St. Louis, Missouri*
If you're a big fan of ginger, this twist on a whiskey sour might be just your thing.

1½ oz. Big O ginger liqueur
1 oz. bourbon or rye whiskey
¾ oz. fresh lemon juice
Glass: rocks
Garnish: lemon zest

Combine all the ingredients in a shaker filled with ice and shake vigorously for 30 seconds. Strain into a chilled glass. Express the lemon zest over the cocktail before floating it on top.

### Ginger Jones
*Great Jones Distillery, New York, New York*
Great Jones is Manhattan's first whiskey distillery since Prohibition, and this cocktail is a gingery treat.

1½ oz. Great Jones rye
½ oz. Barrows Intense Ginger Liqueur
¾ oz. fresh lemon juice
½ oz. simple syrup

3 to 4 oz. ginger beer

Glass: Collins

Garnish: dehydrated lemon wheel and candied
ginger

Pour all the ingredients except the ginger
beer into a shaker filled with a few crushed
ice cubes or 2 or 3 pellets of ice. Shake in a
whip–short-shake manner until the ice is melted.
Double-strain into a Collins glass filled with ice,
top with ginger beer, and add garnish.

**Tart Cherry Sour**

*Liz Henry, co-owner, J. Henry & Sons, Dane,
Wisconsin*

Henry likes to promote local products, so she
uses a tart cherry grenadine simple syrup made
by Quince & Apple in Madison, Wisconsin,
and bitters made in Milwaukee. "Door County
cherries are a big deal in Wisconsin, and this
syrup uses them. It tastes just like tart cherries.
Originally, this was a seasonal cocktail we
served in the summer, but now it's a year-round
drink."

2 oz. J. Henry & Sons small-batch bourbon

¾ oz. Quince & Apple tart cherry grenadine
simple syrup

¾ oz. lemon juice

1 oz. egg white

3 dashes Bittercube cherry bark vanilla bitters

Glass: rocks or coupe

Garnish: 2 Filthy Black Cherries and a lemon
twist

Place all the ingredients except the bitters in a shaker and shake for 30 to 60 seconds. Add ice and shake for another 30 to 60 seconds. Double-strain into a rocks glass with ice or a chilled coupe without ice, carefully add bitters on top, and then add garnish.

**Farmer's Cocktail**
*Liz Henry, co-owner, J. Henry & Sons, Dane, Wisconsin*
Not every visitor to J. Henry & Sons distillery is a fan of whiskey or bourbon. "We have the bourbonphiles who know exactly what they want to try, and we have a lot of first-timers who are just checking the distillery out," says Henry. "And then we have the hostages. They're not here because they want to be here—they're here because some-one important to them wanted to come. They're not grumpy, but they don't enjoy brown liquor or whiskey, and I wanted to give them something they could enjoy." This is a cross between a Kentucky lemonade and a mint julep. Henry says, "They usually ask for seconds."

1½ oz. J. Henry & Sons small-batch bourbon
½ oz. mint simple syrup (see the recipe for basic herbal simple syrup in chapter 4)
4 oz. lemonade
Glass: rocks or mason jar
Garnish: fresh sprig of mint

Place all the ingredients in a shaker filled with ice and shake for 30 seconds. Strain into a rocks glass filled with ice. Spank a long mint sprig between your hands and use it to garnish the drink.

**Color-Changing Sour**
Butterfly pea tea changes color when acid is added. For dramatic flair, the lemon juice is poured over the cocktail.

2 oz. whiskey
¾ oz. butterfly pea tea syrup (see the recipe in chapter 4)
¾ oz. fresh lemon juice
1 dash orange bitters
Glass: rocks
Garnish: lemon twist

In a cocktail shaker filled with ice, shake together whiskey and butterfly pea tea syrup. Double-strain into a rocks glass filled with ice. Add a dash of orange bitters to the lemon juice, pour it over the cocktail, and stir. Watch as it changes color. Garnish with a lemon twist.

**Smoky Sour**
If you have a cocktail smoker, you can add smoke to your whiskey sour, which usually impresses guests.

2 oz. scotch or American single-malt whiskey
¾ oz. lemon juice
¾ oz. simple syrup
½ oz. fresh egg white or aquafaba

2 or 3 dashes chocolate bitters
Mezcal
Glass: rocks
Garnish: smoke

Place all the ingredients except the bitters and mezcal in a shaker filled with ice and dry-shake for 30 seconds. Add ice and shake for another 30 seconds. Double-strain into a rocks glass. Drop bitters on top; then spritz the drink with mezcal using an atomizer or spray bottle. Take a cocktail smoker, aim smoke into the glass, and trap it inside with a glass topper. Remove the topper and serve.

Note: Alternatively, you can smoke the glass first and then pour the cocktail into it.

**Fall into Autumn Sour**
2 oz. bourbon
½ oz. fresh lemon juice
¼ oz. apple cider
¾ oz. rich aromatic syrup (see the recipe in chapter 4)
2 or 3 dashes Angostura bitters
Glass: rocks
Garnish: apple wedge and cinnamon stick

Place all the ingredients in a shaker filled with ice and shake for 30 seconds. Double-strain into a rocks glass filled with ice and add garnish.

**Yuzu and Fig Sour**

*Nelly Buleje, executive chef, Grand Geneva Resort, Geneva, Wisconsin*

Buleje revamped the entire cocktail program at this Wisconsin resort, and this is one of his most popular cocktails.

1½ oz. Suntory Japanese whisky
½ oz. Yakami Orchards yuzu juice
½ oz. house-made sour mix (or equal parts lemon and lime juices)
¾ oz. fig purée or fig jam
1 oz. rosemary syrup
¼ oz. egg whites
Glass: martini
Garnish: dehydrated lemon wheel and edible flower

Place whisky, yuzu juice, sour mix, fig purée, and rosemary syrup in the larger half of a shaker. Place egg whites in the smaller half. Froth the egg whites for 15 seconds, or dry-shake all the ingredients together for 15 seconds. Add 3 ice cubes to the shaker and shake vigorously until they melt. Double-strain into a glass and add garnish.

**Apple-Mint Sour**

*Lisa Laird Dunn, chief operating officer and global ambassador, Laird & Company, Colts Neck Township, New Jersey*

Best described as an apple whiskey, Laird's Applejack is a blend of apple brandy and neutral grain spirit, which adds a touch of apple to any whiskey sour.

2 oz. Laird's Blended Applejack
¾ oz. fresh lemon juice
¾ oz. simple syrup
2 fresh mint sprigs
Glass: martini or coupe
Garnish: mint sprig

Place all the ingredients in a shaker and muddle the mint sprigs. Add ice and shake for 30 seconds. Double-strain into a chilled glass. Lightly slap or spank the mint sprig before adding as garnish.

Note: This cocktail can be made with Laird's Jersey Lightning, which is like moonshine. Angostura bitters and egg white can also be added.

### Lady Laird

*Lisa Laird Dunn, chief operating officer and global ambassador, Laird & Company, Colts Neck Township, New Jersey*

This fresh twist on a whiskey sour sings with muddled sage.

2 oz. Laird's Blended Applejack
½ oz. orange liqueur
¾ oz. fresh lemon juice
½ oz. simple syrup
1 egg white
4 sage leaves
Glass: coupe or martini
Garnish: sage leaf

Place all the ingredients except the egg white in a shaker and muddle the sage leaves. Add the egg white and dry-shake for 10 to 20 seconds. Add ice and shake for another 30 seconds. Double-strain into a chilled glass and add garnish.

**Yuzu Sour**
*The Perfect Purée, Napa, California*
This is a very sweet version for those who don't enjoy the more traditional whiskey sour. For a less sweet and more boozy cocktail, use 2 oz. whiskey and eliminate the simple syrup.

1 oz. whiskey
1¾ oz. The Perfect Purée Yuzu Luxe Sour Blend, thawed
¼ oz. simple syrup
5 dashes orange or Angostura bitters
Glass: martini or coupe
Garnish: 2 cherries

Place all the ingredients in a shaker filled with ice and shake vigorously for 30 seconds. Pour into a chilled glass and add garnish.

**Whistle Bit**
*Five Nine Bourbon, Owensboro, Kentucky*
This is a twist on a whiskey shot and beer combo. The recipe makes 2 cocktails.

2 oz. Five Nine bourbon
½ oz. fresh lemon juice
1 teaspoon honey
2 dashes bitters

2 8 oz. bottles or cans lager
Glass: pint
Garnish: lemon slices or wheels

Place bourbon, lemon juice, honey, and bitters in a shaker filled with ice and shake for about 60 seconds, or until the honey dissolves. Divide the cocktail between 2 glasses, top with beer, and add lemon slices.

### Warden 1854

*Frey Ranch Distillery, Fallon, Nevada*
The Frey family has been farming in Nevada since 1854. Today, they not only grow grains but also use them to make whiskeys in their distillery, which is located on the family farm. This cocktail is a delicious riff on the Ward 8 (see chapter 5).

2 oz. Frey Ranch straight rye whiskey
½ oz. lemon juice
½ oz. grapefruit juice
½ oz. Liquid Alchemist strawberry syrup or homemade strawberry syrup (see the recipe in chapter 4)
1 dash aromatic bitters
Glass: coupe
Garnish: grapefruit peel

Combine all the ingredients in a shaker filled with ice and shake for 30 to 60 seconds. Double-strain into a chilled glass and add garnish.

**New Dancin' Boots**

*The Virginian Lodge and Saloon, Jackson, Wyoming*
This whiskey sour riff is the bar's signature cocktail. It was inspired by the idea of presenting the cowboy persona in a modern light.

2 oz. Wyoming whiskey
1 oz. spiced orange syrup (see the recipe in chapter 4)
1 oz. fresh lemon juice
Glass: cowboy boot or rocks
Garnish: orange twist and sprinkle of cinnamon or cinnamon stick

Pour all the ingredients into a shaker filled with ice and shake for 30 seconds. Double-strain into a glass filled with ice and add garnish.

**The Marriage of Colleen and Alex**

My cousin Colleen asked me to create a signature cocktail for her wedding to Alex. I combined their two favorite whiskeys with Colleen's favorite cocktail, the French 75.

1 oz. single-malt scotch
1 oz. bourbon
4 to 6 marionberries, blackberries, or blueberries
2 dashes orange bitters
¾ oz. simple syrup
¾ oz. lemon juice
3 to 4 oz. champagne or sparkling wine
Glass: champagne flute
Garnish: lemon twist and berry

In the bottom of a cocktail shaker, muddle together scotch, bourbon, berries, bitters, simple syrup, and lemon juice. Shake for 30 to 60 seconds. Double-strain into a champagne flute, top with champagne, and add garnish.

**Apple Sour**
*Peter Kalleward, mixologist, Destination Kohler, Kohler, Wisconsin*
Kalleward created this apple-centric sour in honor of the Normandy Room of the Immigrant Restaurant in the American Club. It's a delicious autumnal sour.

1 oz. Russell's Reserve bourbon or other bourbon
1 oz. apple liqueur
¾ oz. Calvados or other apple brandy
½ oz. St. George spiced pear liqueur or other pear liqueur
⅛ oz. Ancho Reyes chile liqueur
1 oz. fresh lemon juice
1 large scoop (about 1 tablespoon) apple butter

Glass: old-fashioned
Garnish: apple slice or dehydrated apple slice

Place all the ingredients in a shaker filled with ice and shake for 60 seconds. Double-strain into a glass filled with ice and add garnish.

## Lemonheads Sour

*Nick Nagele, cofounder, Whiskey Acres, DeKalb, Illinois*

This is kind of a lowbrow, highbrow cocktail. Whiskey Acres is a "seed to glass" farm distillery that grows its own grains and controls every step of the whiskey-making process, and Lemonheads is a sugary candy. When Ferrara Candy Company opened a factory in DeKalb, Nagele decided to make a cocktail in honor of Whiskey Acres' newest neighbor. Regardless of how much lemon juice you use, this is a very tart sour. You can try variations using other candies such as Sour Patch Kids or gummies.

2 oz. bourbon (preferably Whiskey Acres bourbon)
¾ oz. Lemonheads syrup (see the recipe in chapter 4)
½ to ¾ oz. fresh lemon juice
2 dashes Angostura bitters
Glass: coupe or rocks
Garnish: Lemonheads candies

Pour all the ingredients into a shaker filled with ice and shake for 30 seconds. Double-strain into a glass filled with ice and add garnish.

### Wild Buffalo

*Ishnala Supper Club, Wisconsin Dells, Wisconsin*

Ishnala is one of the most popular supper clubs in Wisconsin, and although it serves 100,000 or more Wisconsin old-fashioneds every year, this new version of the whiskey sour is a big seller too.

2 oz. Ishnala bourbon
1 oz. Gran Gala orange liqueur
1 oz. fresh orange juice
½ oz. fresh lemon juice
2 dashes Angostura bitters
Glass: old-fashioned
Garnish: orange twist

Pour all the ingredients into a shaker filled with ice and shake for 30 seconds. Double-strain into a glass filled with ice and add garnish.

### Pumpkin Spice Sour

Bourbon tastes great in a pumpkin pie, so it makes sense that pumpkin tastes great in a whiskey sour.

2 oz. bourbon
1 oz. rich aromatic syrup—pumpkin spice variation (see the recipe in chapter 4)
¾ oz. fresh lemon juice
1 tablespoon pumpkin purée
¾ oz. fresh egg white
Glass: coupe or martini
Garnish: 3 dashes Angostura orange bitters and sprinkle of pumpkin pie spice

Place all the ingredients in a shaker and shake for 30 to 60 seconds. Add ice and shake for another 30 seconds. Double-strain into a chilled glass and add garnish.

Note: Rub a lemon wedge around the rim of the glass and then dip it into a mixture of sugar and pumpkin pie spice for a more dramatic presentation.

**Tiki Sour**
*Matt Hiel, Wollersheim Distillery, Prairie Du Sac, Wisconsin*
Mixologist Hiel is a big fan of tiki, but the distillery where he works doesn't make rum, so he came up with this lovely cocktail.

2 oz. Wollersheim bourbon
¾ oz. lime juice
¾ oz. passion fruit syrup
Glass: rocks
Garnish: orange slice skewered around an
    Amarena cherry

Place all the ingredients in a shaker filled with ice and shake for 30 to 60 seconds. Strain into a glass and add garnish.

Note: Trader Vic's and Alchemist make great passion fruit syrups.

# Index

Whiskey Stone Sour, 137
Whiskey Strong Yet Sour
    Whiskey Sour, 34
whisky, 102, 135, 147
Whistle Bit, 149
Wild Buffalo, 154
wine: cabernet sauvignon, 131;
    rosé, 125; sherry, 125; shiraz,
    135; sparkling, 151. *See also*
    champagne

Wisconsin Whiskey
    Old-Fashioned Sour, 103
Wisconsin Whiskey Slush, 104
Word of Advice, 139

Yuzu and Fig Sour, 147
Yuzu Sour, 149

zest, citrus. *See individual fruit
    flavors*